Open Go      *)*

Open Government, Open Diplomacy

Conversations with a Former American Diplomat
M. André Goodfriend

ISTVAN HARGITTAI

Central European University Press
Budapest—Vienna—New York

Published in 2023 by
Central European University Press

Nádor utca 9, H-1051 Budapest, Hungary
Tel: +36-1-327-3138 or 327-3000
E-mail: ceupress@press.ceu.edu
Website: www.ceupress.com

Cover illustration: Signing a Hungarian-US agreement with the Hungarian parliament building in the background. André Goodfriend is in the front on the left. The image was generated from the "Night Cafe AI Art Generator" (https://creator.nightcafe.studio) using an original photo as a model.

Cover and book design by Sebastian Stachowski

ISBN 978-963-386-608-5 (paperback)
ISBN 978-963-386-609-2 (ebook)

LIBRARY OF CONGRESS CATALOGING-IN-PUBLICATION DATA

Names: Goodfriend, M. André, interviewee. | Hargittai, István, interviewer.
Title: Open government, open diplomacy : conversations with a former American diplomat M. André Goodfriend / István Hargittai.
Description: Budapest, Hungary : CEU Press, 2023. | Includes bibliographical references and index.
Identifiers: LCCN 2023015705 (print) | LCCN 2023015706 (ebook) | ISBN 9789633866085 (paperback) | ISBN 9789633866092 (pdf)
Subjects: LCSH: Goodfriend, M. André--Interviews. | Diplomats--United States--Interviews. | Democracy. | Diplomacy | Hungary--Politics and government--21st century. | United States--Foreign relations--Hungary. | Hungary--Foreign relations--United States. | BISAC: POLITICAL SCIENCE / International Relations / Diplomacy
Classification: LCC E901.1.G66 A5 2023 (print) | LCC E901.1.G66 (ebook) | DDC 327.730092--dc23/eng/20230418
LC record available at https://lccn.loc.gov/2023015705
LC ebook record available at https://lccn.loc.gov/2023015706

Contents

Preface

Istvan Hargittai

André Goodfriend, who led the US embassy in Budapest for about a year and a half from 2013 to 2015, was seen by many as a folk hero and by others as public enemy number one. When he was originally given the Budapest assignment, playing such a public role was not what he had envisioned; however, the United States was without an ambassador in Budapest when he arrived. He had been a diplomat for a long time and knew that the absence of an ambassador does not mean the absence of leadership.

Goodfriend was born in Los Angeles. His father came to America after World War II as a child, with his family, as refugees from war-torn Europe. His mother was born in the US to immigrant parents. André grew up a true American youth with a diverse European cultural background. His university studies included numerous languages and religious studies, resulting in four undergraduate degrees: Classical Greek, French, philosophy, and radio and television. He later completed his master's studies in mass media, focusing on government use of media. He exchanged his doctoral studies for diplomatic service when offered the opportunity. Prior to Budapest, he was posted to Israel, India, Russia, Britain, Syria, DC, and regionally within Africa. The Budapest assignment, as Deputy Chief of Mission, thus, serving under an ambassador to coordinate the work of the embassy and ensure its smooth operation, was what he was expecting. He was looking forward to putting his work on transparent information sharing and collaborative leadership into practice.

In the absence of an ambassador, however, especially when it became clear that one was unlikely to be sent any time soon, Goodfriend's role changed. He seemed to enjoy the more public, diplomatic role. While he was running the US embassy, we met twice at different events and talked a little. One such occurrence was when, at the invitation of the President of the Central

European University (CEU), John Shattuck, I gave a talk in January 2014 on the comparison of the American Los Alamos and the Soviet Arzamas-16 nuclear laboratories in the context of the publication of my book on Soviet scientists.[1] André Goodfriend was sitting in the front row of the audience. Shattuck introduced us and we engaged in the usual superficial conversation. We agreed to continue sometime in the future over coffee. It didn't work out. The other occasion, a little later, was at an anniversary dinner for a Hungarian-American scholarship organization. I had previously been a member of the board of trustees of the organization and was invited. Goodfriend also spoke at the event; it was at the beginning of his more high-profile diplomatic engagement. His criticisms concerning constraints on civil society, the importance of diversity and inclusion in society, and the corrosive impact of the lack of transparency were expressed in a rather terse manner. We spoke at length at the time because I wanted to make sure that I correctly understood his message. Again, we agreed to have coffee and that didn't work out either. Then my wife, Magdi (short for Magdolna), and I went to America for several months and when we returned to Budapest, Goodfriend was either already packing or had just left.

I knew that in the meantime Goodfriend had become a celebrity in Budapest and his appearances were in line with what I remembered from the anniversary dinner—only now he was expressing his perspective more directly. I also read about a few things during our stay in the United States. For example, that the US embassy had issued a statement condemning the unveiling, by far-right elements of the Hungarian political spectrum, of a bust of Nazi ally Miklós (Nicholas) Horthy in Budapest on 3 November 2014. The Americans saw the need for the statue to be condemned swiftly, firmly, and unequivocally by the highest-ranking Hungarian leaders. This did not happen. Incidentally, in 2017, the Prime Minister's statement praising Miklós Horthy raised eyebrows.

The most memorable moment of André's activities came when the United States announced that six officials affiliated with the Hungarian government would not be allowed to enter the United States because of their involvement in corruption. The names of the six persons, who were not top officials, were

---

[1] Istvan Hargittai, *Buried Glory: Portraits of Soviet Scientists* (Oxford: Oxford University Press, 2013).

not disclosed. However, it soon emerged that one of them was the head of the national tax office, who made a public spectacle of herself. She set out, purportedly, to contact the top US diplomat, André Goodfriend, to clarify why the US government had taken this action toward her. What happened looked as if it had been a choreographed burlesque. The tax chief was accompanied by her lawyer. On her way to the US embassy she was met, as if by accident, by Goodfriend in Liberty Square. According to Goodfriend, he was just taking advantage of the fine weather to go for a walk. The scene was captured on video by one of the pro-government news channels, which just happened to be there, and received a huge number of views on the Internet. The climax of the scene was when the tax chief demanded an interpreter to make herself understood and to understand what Goodfriend might have said to her. The whole affair, including this episode, caused quite a stir in Hungary. Both pro-government and opposition media became preoccupied with who the other five officials might have been and what evidence the Americans might have had of their corruption. This was, in my opinion, a misreading of the situation. The action could have only one purpose: it was a warning. If the corruption cases of these not-so-top officials were being closely followed by the Americans, how much would they know about the corruption involvement of the supreme leader?

I regretted that Goodfriend and I did not have the opportunity for our coffee in Budapest. The next time Magdi and I were in New York, in the summer of 2015, to gather material for our new book, *New York Scientific*,[2] I let him know we were there. He came up from Washington to New York and we finally had a good chat. Our conversation was so engaging that it occurred to me that such a conversation might be of interest to others. That is how the idea for this book was born. To do this, or rather to be formally interviewed "on the record" so that we could write the book, Goodfriend required permission from the US State Department, as he was still in government service. He soon received permission with the stipulation that he would have to submit the manuscript to State Department scrutiny before the book could be published.

We went to Goodfriend's residence near Washington, D.C., in Arlington, Virginia, for two days and he came to our son Balazs's house in Pennsylvania

---

2   Istvan Hargittai and Magdolna Hargittai, *New York Scientific: A Culture of Inquiry, Knowledge, and Learning* (Oxford: Oxford University Press, 2017).

for two days. This was followed by intense correspondence until the manuscript was written. Neither of us thought that a book of such comprehensiveness, substance, and of normal length could come together, but it did. Goodfriend submitted the finished English manuscript to the State Department for review. We were already planning on having a Hungarian translation based on the hoped-for approved manuscript. The State Department took much longer to review the material than I could have imagined necessary. The decision was to not publish the book; however, there were no specific objections. The decision was, of course, valid only as long as André remained in government service.

For quite some time following this, I was able to share only the experience of the conversation with others; not the content. I could say that I had asked someone questions, argued with and provoked someone who was as well prepared as possible for such an exchange, and, who, moreover, articulated himself brilliantly. Though not answering every question to the depth I would have liked, he never brushed off any question or comment, nor missed the point. I thought that Goodfriend should teach open government and open diplomacy at a university; however, I do not know if such a subject is taught anywhere with this or any similar title.

Since then, we have met several times, in Budapest, New York, and Washington. On one occasion I was able to get an impression of how vividly the memory of his activities in Hungary still lives in the "Hungarian mind." In October 2015, I was giving a lecture at the Hungarian Consulate General in New York with Magdi on our joint book, *Budapest Scientific*,[3] organized by the New York Hungarian Scientific Society. The Consulate General had hosted my lectures before. Goodfriend came up from Washington to attend the presentation and attracted more interest from the audience than me, the lecturer. On hearing of his appearance, the Consul General joined the audience and asked Goodfriend how it happened that he was attending this event. Goodfriend said that we had known each other. Two years later, when the possibility of my next lecture at the Consulate General arose, again organized by the New York Hungarian Scientific Society, the Consulate General was silent, and the lecture did not take place, as if I had become persona non grata for the Consulate General.

---

3 Istvan Hargittai and Magdolna Hargittai, *Budapest Scientific: A Guidebook* (Oxford: Oxford University Press, 2015).

The last time André and I met in person was in November 2017, when he came to the American Physical Society's headquarters near Washington, D.C., where Magdi and I both gave a talk. Since then, we have stayed in contact by e-mail correspondence. He has continued addressing issues of modern diplomacy and organizational culture in the changing United States context in a responsible capacity and with his usual total dedication. When the date of his retirement from the Foreign Service was set, we decided to publish our book as soon as it happened. We both re-read the manuscript with an eye to how timely it remained, and we both concluded that it was timelier than ever.

Much of the period between the original conversations and the publication of the book had been dominated by the four years of Donald J. Trump's presidency. We witnessed the attempts to dismantle American democracy and its institutions. In January 2021, after Trump had been defeated in the November 2020 elections, a coup-like attack was launched on America's democratic system and the democratic transition of power. For me, personally, the four years of Trump were a shock, because many of the achievements of democracy that I had admired, and had always missed in Hungary, seemed to have been lost or threatened. I will mention one example here. During conversations with Goodfriend, it was stressed that in America, truth must be told. This is demonstrated in the legal system by the fact that perjury is very severely punished. Likewise, if you lie before federal investigators or a committee of the House of Representatives, there are very serious consequences. When politicians lie in a public appearance, they can be exposed and placed in a very awkward position. However, during the four years of Trump, lying seemed to have become common place in American politics, and Trump and his supporters have continued this practice ever since. They lie about the sacred foundation of American democracy, the elections, because they cannot accept that they lost. They have shattered something that shone and set an example, and in doing so, they cast doubt on those around the world who have held up American democracy as a role model. This is why what is happening in the United States during these years has had significance far beyond America. We must not forget this when we reflect on what is contained in the conversations we are sharing below.

Beyond their general and almost timeless message, the conversations capture a snapshot of the Hungarian political reality in 2014–2015. Much of what happened later in the dismantling of democratic institutions was unimaginable to many at the time. There was still plenty of room for further deterioration, for an increasingly autocratic political leadership, for moving further to the extreme right. I will mention one example here: in 2014, the National Policy Institute in the United States, considered by many to be xenophobic and racist, wanted to organize a conference on "European Identity and the Future of Europe" in Budapest, with the help of the Jobbik Party, which was, at the time, at the extreme right. The event was banned by the Ministry of the Interior on the grounds that it incited hatred. Some foreign organizers were arrested, detained, and deported upon arrival on Hungarian territory. At the time, the US Chargé d'Affaires, André Goodfriend, while noting that the US supports freedom of expression and would probably have permitted such a conference, was pleased to note that the Hungarian government shared concerns that the ideals promoted by the group in question were repugnant. He welcomed the Hungarian government's refusal to support those who promoted racial and ethnic intolerance.[4] This was in 2014. In contrast, in 2018, the government itself organized an event very similar in nature to the conference it had banned in 2014. The most prominent participant of the event was the infamous Steve Bannon, former chief strategist of the Trump campaign.[5] By the way, 2018 was not the end of anything. The process did not stop, and in 2021, Prime Minister Viktor Orbán and his regime could be held up as a role model for the antidemocratic movement in the United States by a notorious anchor of the notorious Fox television network. So, as far as the Hungarian reality is concerned, these conversations provide an authentic snapshot of 2014–2015. André and I believe that this snapshot conveys an enlightening message, not only for today in 2023, but probably also for the future and a growing readership.

---

4   Jared Taylor, "Report from Budapest," *American Renaissance*, October 5, 2014, https://www.am-ren.com/news/2014/10/report-from-budapest/.

5   http://europajovojev4.eu/en/#home (accessed August 30, 2021).

Preface

ANDRÉ GOODFRIEND

Eight years have passed since Istvan and I sat down for the conversations captured in this book. In many ways, it was a thought-provoking conversation between friends about the value of conversations and human engagement, whether in diplomacy or any human endeavor. In many of his previous works, Istvan has drawn on conversations and narratives to connect science and the environment around us with the human stories that underpin and shape our society. This was the thread that connected our conversations as well—afternoon conversations between two people who value the role of humans in shaping society, and who have put that perspective into practice in their professional lives. This focus on the human element, rather than on the shell game of events that flit across our screens, has kept our conversations relevant, despite the years that have passed.

The world of 2023 seems like a vastly different place than that of 2015. Eight years ago, Istvan and I talked at length about the importance of having an open government that valued transparency and engaged collaboratively with its citizens and civil society. At the time, at least on the surface, the political trajectory in the US seemed to favor liberal democracy and a strong civil society. However, there were also other political winds blowing. At about the same time as our conversations, the Open Government Partnership (OGP), a government/civil society partnership that promotes transparent, participatory, inclusive, and accountable governance, began a review of Hungary's membership because of concerns raised by civil society organizations regarding their space to operate in the country. In December 2016, as if to make a point that open government was no longer its societal aspiration; the government of Hungary left the OGP. Also in 2016, Great Britain voted to leave the European Union and the US presidential election dramatically changed the course of American politics. As populist movements gained strength, it seemed that the trajectory of politics throughout the world was changing, moving away from alliances and conversations about shared prosperity toward a zero-sum game in which there could only be one winner. Xenophobia and walls to separate seemed to be replacing compassion and bridges to connect. Societies had become so increasingly polarized, that the consensus necessary for a democracy to function seemed increasingly difficult to achieve.

Then, in 2020, a global pandemic devastated the lives of many and reshaped the way we work, relax, and interact with family and friends. International travel stopped for over a year. In the midst of this physical isolation, communication and easy access to information became increasingly important. Technophiles and technophobes were forced to meet online rather than in person. However, despite the physical isolation and political divisions, people seem to be talking and writing to each other even more than before. Politicians, diplomats, activists, grandparents, parents, grandchildren, and friends use a range of "apps" on their computers and their phones, from wherever they might be to talk "face to face." This brings us back to the importance of conversations.

In all that has been taking place, our ability to communicate, to access credible information, and to understand the conversations taking place has become increasingly important. Private citizens, commercial enterprises, civil society, and governments rely on access to data to compare food prices, to know when the next bus is coming, to assess which neighborhoods are safe, to check what the physical pain they are feeling might mean, to plan travel, to see how their taxes are being spent, to hear the latest music, to keep in touch with family and friends, to gossip, to find out what is happening in the world around them, and much more.

While the ephemeral political winds seemed to be blowing one way and then another, our societies continue to move forward; demanding access to more and more data, whether in closed authoritarian systems or systems that profess to be open. It is increasingly difficult for governments and organizations to stop the flow of data. To do so could risk economic collapse and civil unrest. Individuals are now live-streaming their individual musings or their participation in mass protests. Think tanks, universities, religious institutions, and political organizations, for example, are live-streaming their events, reaching far more people than had ever been possible in a physical room. Radio stations forced off the public airwaves are finding new homes online. That being said, we can be paralyzed by an overabundance of data, and divided by our distrust of the data we encounter. We turn to friends and to those whose opinions we respect to help us sift through "the over-abundance" and interpret what we're seeing. We share links to news stories, amusing videos, and other content, seeking to generate discussion or simply share an experience. Civil society organizations and governments, which want to be seen as entities whose opinions are respected and needed, have to be participants in the conversations that help us interpret the information we see. That was true in 2015 and it remains true with even greater urgency today, as the political winds seem to be shifting again.

Istvan asks questions that inspire thoughtful responses. With every response, I dug deep to provide my sincere perspective. And that's part of the conversation too. Sharing perspectives, and perhaps coming to an answer together.

Innovative Diplomacy

To some, you were a folk hero in Hungary, and still are; to others, you were Public Enemy No. 1. Altogether, you spent some eighteen months in Budapest, which is a short time or long time depending on one's perspective. Could you characterize what you found when you arrived and what it was that you were leaving behind when you were departing?

Let me start by backing up even a little bit more. I would like to talk a little about the importance of conversations; the importance of communicating. As a diplomat, I am not simply broadcasting the government's perspectives via communications media to some anonymous group of people in the distance. As diplomats, we are human beings who are sent by our government to other countries to interact personally, to have conversations, and to talk with representatives of the receiving government directly. These conversations with representatives of the receiving government often take place in private, in closed rooms, discussing issues relating to the relationship between our countries. We discuss government policy, and even joke as we build rapport and come to an understanding at a personal level. It is also increasingly the case, particularly in democracies, that we engage with the public directly. The source of power really is the people; the people vote for the government and governments have to clear their policies, to vet their policies with their citizens. They have to engage their citizens in discussions about policy, and see whether or not they approve it. In this modern democratic environment, where it is expected that private citizens play an increased role in shaping governmental policy, it is increasingly the role of diplomacy to talk directly to citizens. So, in my case, as a diplomat, my role includes explaining the US position, not just to the government, but also to the citizens of the country where

I am residing, so that the citizens might also understand why the US is taking a particular position. This often helps the local government discuss positions that it shares with the US more effectively with its citizens, and therefore work more effectively with us. We hope that the citizens and the government will agree about our shared vision if we have been able to speak effectively about this with both the government and the citizens. Public discussion of US policy is an element of transparency, public participation, and open government.

But this is not what diplomats usually do.

I think the situation has changed. The time has changed. If you look at what were the possibilities decades ago, you'll see that diplomats had fewer opportunities to engage with the public. The mass media were primarily the newspapers. Before television and the Internet and even before radio, people received their information from other people they knew and there were more hierarchical divisions within society.

By the mid-twentieth century, the means of telecommunication had greatly improved and even monarchs, let alone elected leaders, had started using radio and television to talk to their subjects. However, leadership has generally used telecommunication as a one-way channel to explain its policies. Yet many, if not most, substantive decisions were still taking place within closed rooms, "smoke-filled rooms," as we would call them in the United States—highlighting the perception that not only did people in positions of power smoke prodigiously, and who were primarily men, but that there was literally an opaque air about decision making. In the 1960s, there was a lot of dissatisfaction with this exclusion of the public from the decision-making process. Certainly, this was the case in the United States. We changed our processes, how we choose our candidates for president in the late 1960s and the early 1970s in order to listen more to the voices of citizens. Throughout Western Europe, there were also protests at the time and a strong middle class wanted to have its voice heard.

As communication technology developed, the United States was broadcasting and other countries were broadcasting around the world via short-wave radio, recognizing that diplomacy was not just two people talking to each other in a room. It also meant explaining policy and perspectives to the public. What is *Voice of America* except for a way to communicate US policy and US perspectives to the citizens around the world? *Radio Free Europe* throughout Eastern Europe was a lifeline for many. It was a source of information that they could not get from their own media. It was not just news; people listened to music, jazz, and they would hear about other programs. They would listen to cultural programs and other programs that would humanize life outside the closed communication circles.

We have come a long way, arriving at today's possibilities to communicate and to be seen as communicating. The Internet is relatively new. People began by primarily using it for e-mail. Then, they started finding discussion groups, news and entertainment on the web, but for some time, it was still difficult for private citizens to see the Internet as a genuine alternative to older media. Now, we have a wealth of means for communication for everybody. People are often bypassing the traditional news media; they are bypassing television, and publishing their own videos, publishing their own thoughts and perspectives. There are some very good writers, some very objective writers, and some that publish nonsense. Private citizens are communicating to mass audiences; and these tools are available to diplomats as well. These tools enable us to communicate with the public in a different, more personal and interactive way than before.

I was not alone in communicating like this with the public. I was not alone among American diplomats; and diplomats of other countries are also using these technologies. I was not alone in using such technologies in Hungary, nor within Syria where I was before. There are many different embassies that have Twitter accounts; and many diplomats engage individually via Twitter and other social media too. Why the conversations that I was having had become as popular as they did, that's a different story. This folk hero aspect is something I'd be interested in having your thoughts on, too.

Yes, but we are talking about your perspective. Suffice it to say, your activities were different from the activities of other diplomats. Perhaps the principal difference was your visibility and your direct engagement with people of great diversity. You went to places, you showed interest, you appeared informed, and all that you did came through as genuine.

Significant aspects of open government are transparency, participation, and collaboration. It is important for representatives of government, including diplomats abroad, to be open and able to engage with the public. Before coming to Hungary, one of the things I set for myself was to talk with as many people as possible and to hear as many voices as possible. I did not want to just look at either one political group or the other. I did not want to be bound just by contacts with this group or that, and engage only at a certain level of society. I did not want to be bound by only talking with people in what some might consider senior positions, but I also wanted to talk with people throughout the full range of society. This was why I tried to study Hungarian before coming to Budapest and this is why the State Department teaches diplomats languages before they go to their posts.

All American diplomats learn the language, but they make very different uses of it.

I like to walk; I like to talk to the people. In every country where I've been, from the very first, I walked through the city. I have served now in Israel, India, Russia, then I came back to the States, and then I went to Frankfurt, serving as a regional officer for our small posts in Africa; more as an advisor to our consuls in those small posts. Then, I was in Britain, in Syria, and in Hungary. In every place, I walked around and talked to people.

Are you saying that the way you performed your duties in Budapest was more your private initiative rather than fulfilling instructions?

All American diplomats are encouraged to talk to the full range of people living in the country where they are assigned. That being said, we all bring our personalities to our work; I enjoy conversations either one-on-one or in small groups, where it's possible to have a genuine exchange of views. This engagement helps me understand what is happening at different levels of society—the influences within the society. It humanizes the society. As I see it, this is an important element of democracy as well. I like to take a classless approach to the society; they are all citizens, they are all people. I am a citizen as well, regardless of my rank, and I want to have a conversation. I want to know what's going on. I want to watch the television programs. I want to read the different newspapers, see what's happening on the Internet, go to cultural events, see the depressed areas, and see the affluent areas as well.

Then, I want to talk with people. And, as I said, this engaged approach is very much in line with how the US sees the role of a modern diplomat.

What has changed is that the available media have grown and developed, providing more options for having these conversations. It is possible now to have a conversation, a real conversation, not just by seeing someone face to face, but also on the virtual networks as well. The key is engaging, not just putting out your perspective and then walking away, but saying something, listening to what the other person or group of people says, and then thinking about it and answering back. This is a real conversation and maybe this is what surprises people: that you can have such a real conversation with a diplomat. You don't have to go to a hall and listen to the person speak and then ask a question, get an answer, and go away. You can talk to them on the street, you can correspond with them via Twitter or on Facebook, and you get an answer. That was the change. This conversation with the public was the change.

This change was for the duration of your eighteen months.

For me, the personal goal is to understand the society and to accurately represent the values of the United States. We are trying to discuss our shared values, to see how we can achieve our common aspirations; and we are always challenging ourselves to do better. Really, within a country, the citizens have to have such conversations and they have to have those conversations with their government. My goal was showing that it's possible to have these kinds of conversations, and that these don't rely solely upon the diplomat who is there at the time. It is part of our role in presenting public engagement as an example of communication within a democracy. It's really not up to the diplomat, the ambassador, or any other foreign diplomat to change the local society and to engage in local politics, it's up to the citizens themselves. One thing maybe, perhaps, that has changed as a result of our engaging, or as a result of the changing technology is that there are now more conversations taking place.

Do you see your role as having shown an example?

This was an example. One thing that we should do as diplomats is provide examples. We try to be examples of the values of our own country. We will ultimately be talking about open government and transparency, but for this, this is what it is an example of.

The question remains whether your activities were a reflection of your own private initiatives or a signal of the generally changing engagement of diplomats; US diplomats, that is? Was it just an episode?

It is a direction that US diplomacy is taking. There are more and more US ambassadors using Twitter accounts. Our ambassador in Kyiv is very active on Twitter and in having these conversations. The State Department is trying to see how best to work with these media. It's not easy. Having conversations is a very human effort and it's not one that everyone takes to in the same way. The more people see examples, the more we as diplomats see examples of our colleagues having these types of conversations, the more you'll see this taking place.

I heard from others (I was not present) about a big gathering where upon hearing about your departure from Hungary, people stood up clapping as an expression of appreciation towards you, and they did not want to stop. I don't think anybody could have accomplished this merely via social media. Maybe it is embarrassing and you are too shy to speak about this, but you did something different, and you made a difference. How much of this had come from your personality, and how much from the instructions with which you had arrived? A comparison comes to mind, which is too much of an exaggeration, yet I cannot help thinking of it. Raoul Wallenberg came to Budapest in 1944 and he accomplished unthinkable deeds in saving lives during a most trying period. He had instructions from the Swedish government but he performed way beyond the call of his instructions.

I never compared myself with Wallenberg. Well, wait, I take that back. For most of my career I worked as a consular officer. I was a vice consul in Tel Aviv and New Delhi, while in Moscow, London and Damascus I was a consul. In Budapest, I wasn't really engaged in consular work, but I was surrounded by the examples of others who had been—whether they be Raoul Wallenberg or Carl Lutz—and, as you referenced in your book *Our*

Lives[6]—the Japanese consul Chiune Sugihara in Kaunas, Lithuania, during the start of World War II. I have heard the stories of what they did and how they in some ways disobeyed their governments in order to save people. They stood out for their human initiative and managed to change history for thousands of people. They showed the human face of being a consul and acted, sometimes setting regulations aside. I've had to think about what I would do in a similar circumstance. I've been in circumstances where I had to deal with people who were desperate, where we knew that the decision we take, the decision *I* make, might save a life, might take someone out of a terrible situation. My focus has always been on whether I can be proud of my actions and my country.

Knowing that I am serving a government that doesn't require me to break regulations in order to do the right thing empowers me. With the support from my government, and through the support of the laws and regulations that are in place—to do the right thing and still follow the law: this has been my perspective throughout my career.

In some countries, I was responsible for countering fraud; trying to stop people from abusing the visa process through fraud in order to go to the United States. In India, for example, I was a fraud-prevention officer; and in Moscow, I was a fraud-prevention officer. Part of my thinking there too was that ignorance can lead to fraud. People who don't think that they can turn to you for an explanation of the law, who don't think that telling the truth to a government official will help them, may turn to people who take advantage of them. Part of the approach that I tried to embed in our system was to be able to explain our policies and to hear what people had to say, to understand them in their cultural context, and then explain to them what might be the best procedure for them and actually follow it through.

This was the case in Syria, for example, towards the end. I was in Syria when we closed the embassy. We tried to find ways to ensure that people that needed to leave, could leave with the appropriate visas. We also had an American population there, which didn't want to leave for a variety of reasons, for example, because they were married to a Syrian and the Syrian did not have a visa, or they didn't want to leave their parents behind. We explained to them that we could issue an immigrant visa to their parents, husband or wife,

---

6   Istvan Hargittai, *Our Lives: Encounters of a Scientist* (Budapest: Akadémiai Kiadó, 2004).

quickly, in just the same amount of time as to issue a non-immigrant visa if they would be honest with us and tell us what it was they wanted to do. We kept our promise. We worked with Washington to see how we could make sure that this process is efficient, secure, and quick so that we could honestly tell people that our system would support them. We had our own employees at the embassy who were also eager to leave Syria and to whom I had to speak as the head of the consular section. I explained, as the situation was becoming worse, what the difficulties would be if they tried to use a visitor visa to live in the United States versus going through the refugee process, versus going as an immigrant, so as to try to ensure that they made the right choice so that there wouldn't be problems later on. Again, we followed through to make sure that these options worked for them and that Washington would assist. We did as good a job as we could for the people who were trying to get out. If we could not see them in Damascus, we saw them in Amman, Jordan, or in Beirut, Lebanon, to let them have access to our processes in a fair way, and to not have any secrets about how they could get to the United States.

I was in Moscow in the mid-1990s, between 1994 and 1997, and the Internet was just starting to be used broadly. It was a few years after the fall of the Soviet Union; it was during the Yeltsin years. Previously, we had given people information in writing about how to apply for a visa. In this pre-Internet era, people saw the visa procedure as opaque, and there was also less incentive for our government officials to explain their processes. Everything was in books and only we had access to those books. A person on the street wouldn't be able to go and see the consular law and what is prescribed with regards to visas and the services we can offer. One of the things that I did change when I was in Moscow as a mid-level official was how we explain our policies. Everything was on paper and we gave this piece of paper to the public and said that the process of issuing a visa was very complex, and essentially told them to trust the consul to make the right decision. I thought that people are smart enough to understand what should be a clear process. If it is too complex, why do we have that process? If we believe in this process, it should be simple and easy to understand. I rewrote our explanation of these processes, saying that the visa process is very straightforward. Here is how it works. Then, when more of our policies were available on-line, rather than hiding those policies from the public, I thought it was important that we should provide the public with links to the same information that we were working with. If they disagreed with us about an interpretation, we could discuss it with them. It should not be perceived as if we had some esoteric information that only we could understand, when, in fact, this information could easily be made available to the general public. This is one of the basic elements of transparency. They could look our policies up, and we could have a meaningful and constructive conversation about what we can do, about what services our government is able to provide to the public. It's that approach that more and more of us have. If you look at how the US government is handling information, and not just the US, but how other democratic governments approach freedom of information, you will see this change that has been taking place over the past twenty years.

Now we are at the point where everyone knows how to access a web site for information. The next stage will be, in a sense, to go back a hundred years, but use these modern technologies to have human conversations with people. Not just give them gray policy and say, read it yourself, but to have a conversation. That's a change; that's something new.

Crisis Prevention

I've read that when there was a crisis somewhere, they would send you there for crisis-prevention.

I volunteer. We all volunteer. That's how it works with crises. It depends on the area of your expertise. For example, Kyiv needed people following the Maidan protests in 2014, so embassies were asked if they had spare officers and if there were people who wanted to help. Whenever there is a crisis, whether it is an earthquake, civil unrest, anything, there may be need for people and the State Department asks for volunteers.

For some reason, this is what I read about you.

I have been places where there were crises, just as the majority of my colleagues have been. I am not sure that we would call Moscow a crisis area.

I can hardly imagine many more important places for US diplomacy than Moscow.

It was one of my top choices as far as places to go. I've always been fascinated by the culture there. Our process for going to places is that different openings are announced and we look over those openings. We choose which ones interest us. As you move to different stages of your career, there will be more availability at lower levels than at higher levels. Moscow has always been a location of interest to me and I was very fortunate that I was there at an interesting time (from 1994 to 1997, following the collapse of the Soviet Union, as Russia came to terms with a new, internal political order).

We had agreed that we would not place too much emphasis on events in Hungary, but my impression is that we are avoiding the topic even beyond what would still not be conspicuous to include. When you volunteered or were sent to go to Hungary, was it considered to be a crisis situation?

When I sought out Hungary as an assignment, it was 2011. It was on the list of availabilities. My predecessor, Tim Betts, was scheduled to leave in 2013. The assignment was on the list of open assignments in the summer of 2011 and the reason that it was so early was because I had to have a year of Hungarian language training. In order to make the preparations, to take language training in 2012, I had to ask for the assignment in the summer of 2011. It was not a matter of choosing to send me to a crisis area. This was an open post and I thought I would do a good job in managing an embassy, but I was also expecting that there would be an ambassador. There was an ambassador in 2011 when I bid on the Budapest position. There was no indication that there would not be an ambassador when I arrived. The fact that there was a gap was a surprise. I arrived in the summer of 2013 and the nomination of Ambassador Bell[7] was announced in November 2013. Even then, there was a sense that perhaps by the end of 2013 there would be an ambassador. The congressional hearing was in January 2014 and then we thought that there would be an ambassador by the spring of 2014. But it did not happen that way. The fact that there was no ambassador, and we could not say when there would be an ambassador—that was one of the reasons that I had to be sure that as the head of the embassy, we did not let our foreign policy suffer. Just because there isn't an ambassador, that doesn't mean that there is not a chief of mission or that the United States is not represented in a country. We could not let the voice of the embassy be silent during that period.

Answering your question directly about the situation that I found arriving in Hungary, I found a country of people who were interesting to talk to. I had come there in March 2013 to practice Hungarian; I was still in a Hungarian class and had gone to different types of places to practice speaking. Every place I went, they did not know who I was, but they welcomed me.

---

7   Ambassador Colleen Bell was appointed by President Barack Obama to serve as the United States' Ambassador to Hungary and was confirmed by the United States Senate in December 2014. Ambassador Bell presented her credentials to President of Hungary János Áder on January 21, 2015 (https://2009-2017.state.gov/r/pa/ei/biog/236916.htm).

Even with my minimal Hungarian at the time, they would have conversations with me. Sometimes they wanted to switch to English, but they were tolerant of me when I said, "No. I am only going to speak Hungarian." *Mondtam, hogy "a cél... hogy nekem kell beszélni magyarul."*[8]

I had begun Hungarian language training in September 2012; and, after I had achieved some proficiency, in March 2013, I came to Hungary for two weeks to practice speaking. It was a sort of immersion with the language. I came on my own, because I was in a very small class and I was the only one who had the opportunity to come. I organized my training in Budapest myself, working a little bit together with the embassy. I went for two hours of structured language training at one of the local Hungarian language schools in Budapest, which provided a classroom setting, but it was one on one with a teacher. We would have conversations mostly for two hours per day.

This was also a good opportunity to learn something about Hungarian society through these conversations. Outside the school, I went to different places. There was a "meetup" group focusing on communication where I went once. There was a folk dancing group that I went to. The members of the group were all Hungarians, and I had to hear all the instructions to dance in Hungarian. I went to the town of Újszász, outside of Budapest, to a high school there and talked to the teachers, the headmaster, and the students, all in Hungarian. I went to a high school in Budapest; they knew I was coming, and they prepared a meeting for me with a class that wanted to practice English. We agreed that I would speak Hungarian and they would speak English. I went to many of these meetings on my own, or accompanied by one person from the embassy. I met with other groups. I met with a Roma group, and went to a Passover Seder. I did a number of different things within Hungary to talk with people. They were very friendly, very willing to talk, and tolerant of my desire to only speak Hungarian. It happened that a group of students was a little frustrated because we could not talk about complicated things and they wanted to be sure that I knew that they could speak English. They still were tolerant and they humored me and let me speak Hungarian with them.

When I came to Budapest in August 2013, I wanted to continue conversations with people. I found a country where people were very open about their opinions, very willing to talk with me and with others about what they

---

8   I told them that "my goal is ... that I practice Hungarian."

thought about their society, what they thought about politics, about their hopes or their fears, but there was not much confidence and there was not much humor. That was my perception. I found an amazing people where there was a sense of history and a sense of pride as well as culture, a lot of creativity, people who were able to do more than they believed they could. But they were not very confident, they did not think people were paying attention outside of Hungary, and they were not stepping back and seeing any humor in their own situation.

Everything was very serious compared to the environment that I was familiar with in the United States, where we seemed to see more humor in our daily situation; there are television programs that take a humorous view of the political situation. We can step back, laugh at our leaders and laugh at ourselves too. People were not laughing very much at themselves in Hungary. They were laughing at other people. Whenever I asked people, "Where is the laughter? Where is the humor?" they said we don't have a tradition of laughing at ourselves and we don't have a tradition of humor in Hungary. I was surprised at hearing that because my understanding was that there was a lot of humor in Hungary during the communist years and in the pre-World War II years. There was a cabaret culture and, during the Kádár years, there was a lot of self-mocking. Once we got into conversations, people remembered that, "yes, we used to laugh a lot during that period," and they would point out the statue of Géza Hofi. They told me to look up some of Hofi's videos on YouTube. So, after all, there was a lot of laughter at their own circumstance. But at the time of my arrival that humor was missing and I was out on a hunt for where the humor was. To be able to understand the nature of society, it is important to understand its humor. The more I looked, the more I did find pockets of humor, including books taking a mocking view of society, and the magazine *Hócipő*. Somehow, people found it hard to acknowledge that there was humor within the society. I don't take myself too seriously and I don't mind having people laugh at me; it's fine, for example, that people were joking about my neckties. This was a very interesting situation. Some of the online services had a competition to vote for the best necktie or to understand hidden codes on the neckties.

There were references to my unexpected meeting with the head of the Hungarian tax authority on Szabadság tér [Freedom square – ed.] and that became a humorous video for many. More and more people are pointing to their own circumstance with some humor. It changed the mood somewhat. The Twitter conversations I was having; many of those conversations were imbued with a little bit of humor. Even with some politicians, there were some humorous discussions on Twitter with regards to Shakespeare or with regards to the hidden meaning of some of the Twitter conversations. Even the billboards that were erected recently with regards to immigration to Hungary carried humor. There were government billboards and there were billboards that were placed by a humorous political party, which required that people take a step back and see some of the humor in the situation and get some strength from that.

This was a change that was taking place in the society through humanizing it a little bit and having conversations where people felt empowered to say what was on their mind.

Could your contribution to this change be the most important impact you had on the situation in Hungary?

I'll let others say what the most important impact I had was. I think recognizing the strength of citizens and their ability to engage with each other and engage with their government, and letting the citizens control the narrative is a big thing in democracy; for the citizens to feel that they can engage the people in power, that they don't have to just be the *hallgató* as the university students are called in Hungarian—"the listener." Another thing people told me was that if you go and give a speech, give a presentation, don't expect that people will ask any questions or enter into a discussion. I talked with students about this and they told me that this was the case; they did not ask questions and they were not encouraged to ask questions. The *hallgató* is supposed to listen. Yet, at the same time they were saying that, they were asking questions, they were engaging. There was a lack of realization that they were in fact more engaged than they thought they were. There is a type of awakening that happens when a person talks with someone and finds that that person is actually listening, there are other people that you can talk with as well, and that you are not alone in the way that you think. You realize that it's not always a grim, serious struggle, but that sometimes it's a very human endeavor in which there are a lot of emotions at play and that you have to acknowledge that.

*I've read that your principal areas of activity, in addition to crisis preven-
tion, are new technologies and open government. Is this a fair characterization?*

Consular work has been my focus for the majority of my career. Consular
work encompasses not so much conflict prevention, but assisting people: the
human element of a situation whether in a crisis or in a conflict—how do we
work with the individual? How do we work with private citizens? Around
the turn of the millennium, 1997 to 1999, after my return from Russia, I
was working on conflict prevention, focusing in particular on the conflict
in Kosovo. During that time, one of the guiding principles for conflict prevention was early warning—early response. One of the reasons why conflict
prevention took on a new life during that time was former UN Secretary
General Boutros Boutros-Ghali's "Agenda for Peace."[9]

After the first Gulf War, when all of these nations had come together in
a large coalition to push back against the incursion by Iraq against Kuwait,
Boutros-Ghali proposed that rather than just responding to attacks, we could
work together through the United Nations to prevent conflict. There was a lot
of discussion; how can we do that? What is the best way to prevent conflict?
There were different groups that came together to study it and come up with
proposals. One of them said, if we only had better warning systems, then we
could respond. I tried to focus less on early warning and early response, but
on how to have an infrastructure always in place that can act a bit more like
preventive medicine. When you try to prevent disease, you don't wait until
you see the signs of an outbreak and then respond quickly. You need an infrastructure that is constantly in place. Healthy people should also see doctors.
People know that there are steps they need to take to prevent disease, especially
when they're healthy. If you see slight indications that might be an indication
of disease, you know what to do. It is the same thing with conflict and this
is what we talk about when we consider the role of civil society and the role
of citizens monitoring their societies, so they can keep their societies healthy.
They want to make sure that there is adequate education, that health care is
good, that the society is monitoring the levels of poverty, and not just wait-

---

9   Boutros Boutros-Ghali (1922–2016) was the 6th Secretary General of the United Nations (1992–
     1996). The United States vetoed his election for a second term.

ing for signs of conflict before responding. That was the focus of conflict prevention at the time.

What we did in Kosovo also dealt with communication and how we understand a situation. We had diplomatic observers in Kosovo. The idea was to let the Serbian government know that we are seeing what is happening there, not just relying upon press accounts, which could be exaggerated, but diplomats themselves are there and seeing what is happening in the field. The information that our government receives is not coming from hearsay and from other parties, but is coming directly from what the diplomats themselves are seeing. This might inhibit either side from engaging in atrocities, if they know that the world is watching what's happening, and the observers can play that role. That was in 1999, before there were smart phones with video cameras all over the place. The idea was similar; if the world is watching, it's harder to commit atrocities. You can see this theme continuing, even now, when we are seeing what's happening around the world, not just by having diplomatic observers there, but by people taking videos and posting them to the Internet where others can see what's happening and try to interpret it. This is also why it's always important for us as diplomats to see things with our own eyes. We walk around and have people know that we are seeing what's happening in a country. This is an important element of diplomacy to keep us all on the right track. Good diplomacy is a big element of conflict prevention.

The Hungarian government often accuses the EU and the United States that they form their opinions about what's going on in Hungary on the basis of false information.

This was one of the things that I talked about in an interview on ATV. There were headlines afterwards in the Hungarian press, which said that the head of the American embassy says that his government receives information about the situation in Hungary from the embassy, as if it were a surprise. In fact, I "tweeted" the following day that: "We draw from facts; and it goes without saying, though it seems it must be said, embassies keep governments informed." The role of diplomats, the role of the embassy is to provide information to its government about the situation in the country. That's why we're there. It's one of the main roles of the diplomats.

People's Diplomat

You were one of the rare diplomats who got into contact with "real" people versus only government officials.

I worked, like all my colleagues do, with a team. The embassy is not just one person going out and presenting his or her observations.

Weren't you doing this more than others?

I was visible, but my colleagues were also doing this. After a while, people were able to recognize me, and they did not see my colleagues, but they were out there. I was more visible because I was interviewed more frequently or because of my Twitter account; the press began to quote that regularly. For a period, in November and December 2014, almost every day you could see something about me in the Hungarian press. That does not mean that my colleagues were not active. When I was out, people saw me. There were even competitions to locate where I was. If I went to a restaurant or went to a movie, went to a place with inexpensive food, sometimes there was a story that I was at that place. The impression was that I was in many, many places.

How did this develop?

It could have a chicken and egg aspect; the more I was expressing US policy on media and public places, the more people focused on me. The more people focused on me, the more they publicized where I was. The more they publicized where I was, the more media focused on me. It built up that way.

I became very much the personal face of US policy within Hungary, which, frankly, is one of the achievements of this attempt to humanize diplomacy.

...And which is usually not accomplished. This is just an observation.

[Long pause] It depends on the circumstances. The reason I'm pausing is that I am trying to think what some of the factors are behind it. The use of social media has changed things significantly. People who use social media, diplomats who use social media, ambassadors who use it, they can achieve more recognition that way.

I'll give you another story from Syria. While I was there, the security situation was deteriorating. We had a responsibility to see about the welfare of American citizens in Syria. It was very difficult for us to go to those places where they lived, or for them to travel. We, nevertheless, would send a consul or a vice-consul to different places where there were American citizens to see what was happening; to see how they were. In some places there were large demonstrations; but even if there was a vice-consul present, nobody paid attention to the vice-consul's visit. Then, the ambassador went to one of the cities, the same one that the vice-consul had visited a month or so earlier. There was a large demonstration and Ambassador Robert Ford went to that city, Hama. This was in July 2011. As soon as people saw the ambassador's car, even if they hadn't recognized the ambassador, they recognized the car. Now, this was something major. They saw the car and they began to celebrate the fact that the chief of mission of the American embassy had come to see what was happening. They threw flowers at the car, they danced around the car, and they put a video about it on YouTube. Even before the ambassador had returned to Damascus, there was already a video of the visit and the celebration about that visit to Hama. This increased the visibility of the ambassador and irritated the Syrian government, and they restricted our travel even more.

This may sound like a cheap shot, but my impression is that sometimes when I ask you about Hungary you bring up an example from Syria. Is there a parallel?

That's a cheap shot. [Laughing] Syria was my previous assignment before Hungary and I'm trying to follow continuity and highlight aspects of recognition and personification of US policy in an individual. So, social media plays a big role in this. The example was that posting a video on YouTube within Syria was equivalent to reaching out directly to the public. The embassy began to communicate to the public extensively via Facebook, because we couldn't get out in other ways. It was very effective and it facilitated discussion among people who had not been able to participate in such a discussion before.

I'm just drawing upon my personal experience. For second-hand experience, you can look around the world and see where our ambassadors are using these modern technologies to engage public discussion. It's not just us. There was recently an article about a British ambassador to Lebanon and his use of a blog to personify his role there. These new technologies make it possible to not have a diplomat just as a gray bureaucratic character, but as a person who engages, who is willing to talk with people, and who makes the embassy accessible. That's something I've tried to do, and I know my colleagues are trying to do. It is something that ultimately becomes a thread of US diplomacy and a thread of our own engagement with our own citizens towards open government.

Another cheap shot: It appears that, ultimately, there was not much success in Syria.

In doing what?

Whatever it was you were trying to achieve.

We were successful in safeguarding the welfare of our citizens, which was my primary role.

Of course, I didn't mean it personally.

As far as preventing the breakdown of the situation or in minimizing the civil unrest, unfortunately, no, that didn't happen. We tried and we're still trying—and this together with a number of other countries, including Hungary—to move towards a negotiated agreement within Syria. Such an agreement would facilitate achieving a peaceful and stable future for a democratically elected government. That is a difficult thing and I'm not working on that now, and I can't speak with any authority about our policy there now. However, to talk about what we were successful at or what we were not successful at in Syria at the time—this was a conflict from 2011 and it's still going on, and we closed our embassy in February 2012.

Prior to 2011, the situation was relatively calm and people felt safe in Syria, because it was a police state. There wasn't a lot of crime on the streets, people felt they could walk on the streets at two in the morning, and they were safe as long as they understood what it meant to live in a police state; just as people who grew up in Eastern Europe under communism felt safe as long as they did not engage in political activity. In Syria, during that time of relative stability, we tried to engage with citizens to have a communication link with them. We were there not just during periods of crises, but during periods when everything was relatively normal. This gets back to the conflict prevention problem. It is not only when there are signs of violence that you start creating the infrastructure. Prior to unrest, one of our consular responsibilities is to engage with American citizens. We did that in Syria. We sent out monthly newsletters, we tried to show that we were there for them whenever they needed us, and that we were open and our doors were open. When the conflict erupted, we already had ways to communicate with our citizens. They could trust us, and we could walk them through the processes of the services that we were still able to provide, and what we were no longer able to provide. We told them why it was that they should leave the country, what routes they can take, and we told them, "You should go now." While we were there, we were able to facilitate their departure—not pay for the departure—advise people and be there as an authoritative voice that they could trust. People took our advice and left Syria.

The American citizens.

Yes.

What we are observing today [2015] *is that many more people are leaving.*

We're observing that and we need to look at the institutionalization of processes. The UNHCR—the UN Refugee Agency (United Nations High Commissioner for Refugees) is there to try to facilitate the refugee flow. The

International Organization on Migration (IOM) is there. There is an infrastructure. There is no general rule for how individual countries deal with displaced people; however, there are international organizations and processes that can help manage this flow of people. This is, again, an example of a situation in which the question is whether you wait for the crisis to develop, or at least try to get an infrastructure in place before it happens.

Foreign Policy Goals

The United States can take only a limited amount of action in faraway lands where events may threaten or endanger democracy. How much should the United States be concerned when it witnesses the dismantling of democratic institutions in a country, like in Hungary?

Again, these things do concern the United States. Secretary of State Hilary Clinton referred to this when she visited Hungary in 2011, as even then there were signs of rolling back democracy. We are looking institutionally at how we work now in the twenty-first century to try to promote democratic principles. After World War I, there was the League of Nations that the United States did not join, although it was the brainchild of the United States. Some of the issues in our democracy with regards to the relationship between the executive branch and the legislative branch and membership in these organizations were contentious even then. There are underlying principles which guide these organizations, and which are generally there to promote stability and prevent war. A goal of the League of Nations, established after World War I, was to prevent a second world war. In these organizations, the member nations would identify shared principles.

The League of Nations failed utterly.

That's right, it failed.

The failure was not only that it could not prevent the conflict; it let it develop and by its inaction, and by the policy of appeasement, it encouraged aggressor nations to action.

We still had to have ideals, visions, some type of ways in which we can take action in a non-haphazard way. The idea that we can identify our shared principles and shared values and work together to try to achieve them, remains a goal. The League of Nations did fail; Germany pulled out, the United States never joined, and there were a number of reasons why it was not able to achieve the goals that it set for itself. We'd hoped that the United Nations after World War II would now be structured in a way that would enable it to prevent conflict. It is still a goal: the goal of global peace.

Let me be more provocative.

Be more provocative.

We have moved away from my original question, but that's alright. The impression is that the United States is more willing to interfere when the problem is in a small country than when it is in a stronger power. What I have in mind is Russia's action in the Ukraine [this was in reference to the annexation of the Crimea by Russia in 2014]. *Are we witnessing a situation that resembles the 1930s, or is it entirely different? Of course, historical analogies are never accurate, but that does not mean that we could not learn from them.*

We have been fairly clear in our characterization of what Russia has been doing and the analogies we can draw are not just the 1930s but also the 19th century.

Referring to the 1930s, I meant Nazi Germany.

Yes, but even if we take Russia, we may find analogies in Russian history in the early twentieth century and the nineteenth century. Russia used its military to carry out foreign policy goals to invade and conquer. It has appeared as if the infrastructure that we, the world, put together in the second half of the twentieth century did not bring the expected benefits. The goal was to make the world a peaceful, prosperous place with more trade, better standard of living, the ability of people to travel, and greater opportunities for advancement because of the infrastructures, because of free trade, because of free movement of people, the recognition of international law, and the agreements between countries that would promote a shared welfare.

Russia has been a valued partner in this international framework. What we have witnessed is the setting of these achievements aside and a return to a destructive focus on ethnic national interests, hegemonic interests, and the use of military force to safeguard them. It is a throwback to a different era. This is a discussion on protecting ethnic communities regardless of what citizenship they may have and that states can expand their authority into other states in order to safeguard their ethnic communities and that the world should be divided along ethnic lines rather than along political state lines. This is a very complicated discussion, which is reminiscent of the late nineteenth century and early twentieth century.

Russia may also have legitimate concerns about what is happening in the Ukraine.

It should be concerned, as should Ukraine's neighbors and as should the United States. Russia should work together within the twenty-first century framework.

The impression is that Russia can do almost what it wants to do.

The rest of the world is trying to counter that. This is why there had been such a unified coalition against the unilateral military actions of Russia in Ukraine [2014]. Certainly, as a neighboring state, Russia has an interest in what happens in the Ukraine. How it goes about safeguarding those interests is where the huge debate is. Russia has chosen safeguarding its interests by sending in its military as opposed to working with its partners to ensure a peaceful stabilization of democracy there: the ability of Ukrainian citizens to choose their own future, to eliminate corruption within their government, to be participants in a modern democracy. Instead, Russia has chosen to take over part of Ukraine.

The countermeasures [in 2014–2015] did not work; they haven't at least so far.

The situation is still ongoing. Russia is not benefiting from this situation. It's holding on tenaciously to what it's managed to occupy. The rest of the world is moving Russia out of the environment in which it had been a partner. It's becoming, in other words, isolated and it is feeling the pain for that.

Is there a red line where the United States would do more than just sanctions?

I'm not going to talk about red lines.

I am not asking you about where the red line is, but should there be a red line?

It's very difficult to talk about red lines; binding yourself to taking an action. Some would say that World War I started with red lines because of the treaty obligations of the participants. If country X attacks country Y, it's a red line.

In contrast, we might say that World War II came to pass because there was no red line opposing Nazi Germany's aggressions and conquests.

If we resort to hypotheticals, we might say that World War II was the continuation of World War I.

There is a red line defined unambiguously; if one of the NATO members is attacked, all NATO members consider themselves under attack.

That is a red line. We have to be cognizant that the NATO countries can be pulled into a war whether they want to be or not, because one of them has been attacked. If there were an attack on any one of the NATO countries, the rest have to respond. The last time was 14 years ago (on September 11, 2001, while this conversation was taking place on September 12, 2015) when there was the terror attack on the US, a NATO country. We appreciated that NATO was with us during that time.

One has to be careful with red lines; President Obama declared a red line concerning the civil war in Syria and did not follow it up.

That's the problem with red lines.

We were talking about conflict prevention.

Considering the conflict prevention model, there are warning signs, however, oftentimes, while waiting for the warning signs to happen, and when they happen, it may be too late to take effective action for the prevention of conflict. Instead of waiting for red lines, the goal should be to identify the things to put in place even before those warning signs would show up. We are still somewhat healthy, but we already know that inevitably, just due to the cycle of things, there will always be somewhere a chance for instability, for disease. How can we monitor ourselves regularly; have structures in place that could prevent it? This gets back to the international organizations and institutions that we have; the role of civil society; the value of partnership between governments and citizens; they all having the ability to constantly monitor the situation. This, then, brings us back to the role of transparency, of open government, of the relationship of citizens between each other and between citizens and government, safeguarding their own security.

Open Government

Open government and transparency are almost synonymous.

Transparency is a big part of open government. Open government also means engaging with citizens. Why should government be transparent? Is it just a glass window for people who have no voice just to be able to see what's happening behind the wall? There may be some value to that, but it's a minimal value, to just let people see what's happening. I am just thinking, some of the conflicts that have arisen around the world happened because people can see what they don't have. They can see things that they can't participate in; it's through television, through films, and through the Internet now. People who are disenfranchised are able to see what others have and they don't have, and they want it. They want to have what they can see.

It's not just about being transparent and not just about showing citizens what the government is doing, but also about engaging citizens, letting citizens know that, yes, we are doing these things and you are a part of it. This is information that you've paid for. We need to be accountable for what we are doing. We are presenting you, giving you this window into your government, because we want you to have a voice. We want you to be able to know what your government is doing and shape the direction of your government. It involves not just showing what's happening, not just freedom of information, but also working with civil society. It requires working with private citizens to find ways to incorporate the input from private citizens. It means encouraging private citizens, encouraging businesses to use the information that their governments are producing to innovate, to become better entrepreneurs, to use information that their taxes are paying for. Open government encourages the private sector to come up with private sector solutions for societal problems and help their government in managing those problems. All this is much more than being transparent.

Is open government considered to be a new discovery?

It's not a new discovery.

Of course, it is not, but the present US Administration has almost presented it as such.

The present Administration launched the Open Government Initiative in 2009, shortly after it took up office. Tools have become available; we have to look at the changing technology of the infrastructure within the world. By 2009, we had moved from Internet 1.0 to Internet 2.0 or www 1.0 to www 2.0. Around that same time, already by 2007 or 2008, the Internet was not simply a one-way communication tool, but could be used more for two-way engagement. This is not just a matter of putting information out, but also engaging with citizens more effectively and using the technologies that exist now to enable governments to do so. This is not just happening in the United States and in Western Europe, but in all democracies that have the same principles, the same ideals.

Getting back to the theme of setting an example, in 2009, this Administration launched the Open Government Initiative. We first created individual cabinet-level ministry plans—department plans—by 2010. Then, in 2011, we created a national plan. At the same time, we said that these are principles of democracy—transparency, accountability, partnerships with citizens – and we're not alone in this. There are other countries that also have these principles that will benefit from working together and from the innovation that open government brings. It is from having that information that governments are making available to citizens that helps spur innovation in commerce, trade, et cetera. In 2011, there was the Open Government Partnership initially with eight countries; now it's up to sixty-six, and one of those partners is Hungary. Each of these countries has presented a national action plan for open government, sharing its best practices and making its information available so that we can work together with common information on addressing some of the problems within our societies.

Had other countries been ahead of the US with respect to the ideals and practices of what you label now as open government?

There were countries that were making information available like us that had different freedom of information laws being passed in this period. Some countries were putting their statistics on-line. Different world organizations, the United Nations, the Organization for Economic Co-operation and Development (OECD), and others, all would publish various reports and statistical information with regards to education levels, poverty, health issues, financial matters, et cetera. There was information increasingly made accessible to the public with the Internet as a framework for it to take place. The questions arise, what are the benefits? What are the values? Why should we be making this information accessible? We should not be just doing it because we can, and not just doing it in a haphazard way, but laying out common principles and saying that openness in government, working with civil society, having accountability, these are things that spur economic development, lead to better governance, and are essential within democracies. Laying out those principles and moving ourselves forward along those lines is something that had not been done before in quite the same way.

Providing information and helping the economy this way, however indirectly, this is understood. Concerning dialog with civil society, however, how do you envision a change or justify the need for a change in the United States where you have democratically elected representatives and senators, and not only has this system been in place for a long time, but it has worked. How would civil society be channeling responses if not through their elected representatives?

With regard to the open government plan, we are putting our working drafts of new legislation or other initiatives on-line and taking suggestions from civil society through the Internet. For example, the National Action Plan is being discussed with different civil society organizations that are interested in transparent government while it's being developed. We are actively seeking the input of civil society on-line for what are the challenges of the initiatives that should be highlighted in this National Action Plan. There is a web site available for the public...

Is this something similar to "National Consultation" in Hungary?

Except that this is transparent. There are different ways of holding national consultations. There is one where you can say, send us your suggestions; the suggestions are going to this box, and we will look at them, and we will tell you what we find. That's a consultation. Then, there is one where you could say, post your suggestions where everybody can see them and comment on them. The discussion is not being handled in a sealed box, but is handled in an open, transparent way. You can see what others have suggested, you can comment on what others have suggested. The discussion is taking place very much in the open. We do this as well with draft legislation where any proposed legislation is made available on the Internet for comment and discussion in public. It is not where comments and suggestions are sent in privately and quietly and reviewed in some place where no one else can see them. There are different models for consultations. We're trying to model transparency, to set an example in working with the public, in the same way that we want our final document to promote transparency and openness. We want the process to reflect the type of goals we are trying to achieve within open government.

Here is just the concluding question of the Hungarian National Consultation about immigration and terrorism. Question No. 12: Do you agree with the Hungarian government that it is necessary to support Hungarian families and unborn children rather than immigration?

☐ *Strongly agree*   ☐ *Rather agree*   ☐ *Disagree*[10]

The composition of this question and the impossibility of a fair response to such a question tells volumes about the people who compiled this questionnaire and the aims and methodology of such a National Consultation. It cannot have anything in common with what you are talking about with regards to the American engagement in discussion with the public.

---

10 "Nemzeti Konzultáció a bevándorlásról és a terrorizmusról." "12) Egyetért-e Ön a magyar kormánnyal abban, hogy a bevándorlás helyett inkább a magyar családok és a születendő gyermekek támogatására van szükség?
    ☐ Teljesen egyetértek   ☐ Inkább egyetértek   ☐ Nem értek egyet"

Social scientists, experts on survey methodology, and even members of the European Parliament have commented at length upon the wording of the questions in Hungary's most recent National Consultation. The concept of open government is not about dictating the wording that should be used on a survey, but rather that there is value to having such as survey, that it is important to engage citizens in shaping government policy. Questions to ask, questions that we in the US ask ourselves as we implement our open government initiatives, are whether the process was as transparent as is could be. Was the public genuinely engaged? Did civil society play a role? We all, within our countries, must ask ourselves these questions. And membership in the Open Government Partnership helps ensure that we keep to our commitments with regard to open government.

For me, it's hard to imagine a less open government than the present one in Hungary [2015]. How can such a partnership work in the open government program?

Each member of the Open Government Partnership puts in a plan and subscribes to the goals, the values of the Partnership. No one is forcing a government to be a member of the Partnership. They join because they subscribe to those goals and they say that they plan not just to follow, but to set the vision, and they say that these aspirations are their aspirations. The civil society organizations that are supposed to be working with the government try to monitor the country's adherence to the goals that they've set; the country's adherence to each country's own National Action Plan. If a country doesn't meet the goals of the plan that it had developed, if it does not follow the principles that it had agreed to, then there is a mechanism within the partnership for people to complain. People can ask that the government be held to account. In July 2015, several civil society organizations in Hungary posted their concerns on-line about Hungary's adherence to its National Action Plan. They submitted their concerns to the Open Government Partnership. There are mechanisms in place to help ensure that the countries meet the principles that they had subscribed to.

What is that mechanism?

Each country puts together a National Action Plan and it is a public document. They are all available on-line. They had been developed together with civil society organizations, and there are principles that all had agreed to as part of the Open Government Partnership as well. If a country is not adhering to those principles, then civil society organizations can identify those areas where the country is not adhering to the agreed commitments, and submit them to the Partnership. This is reviewed by a couple of the other countries to see whether these concerns have merit.

What happens if they do?

Members of this organization are expected to meet their commitments. This is not something where there would be economic sanctions, but if they're not complying with their commitments; it would be pointed out to them. They would have to say that they are not going to do it, in which case you wonder why they are in the organization. Again, this is an organization which countries choose to belong to.

What if they want to belong in order to pretend that they subscribe to the principle of the Partnership whereas in reality they don't?

By belonging to the Partnership they have made their commitments. When you say their purpose may be to show something that's not there, this is where this mechanism comes into place. If the complaints are valid, that would be pointed out.

And then?

If they are showing something that is not there, it could affect the country's continued participation in the Open Government Partnership. If you are in a club where everyone is supposed to wear a red shirt, and you decide that you want to wear a green shirt and you start coming to the club in a green shirt, even though you had said you would be coming in a red shirt, someone might ask you, why are you wearing a green shirt? You have to decide. If you can't abide by your commitments to the organization, the question arises, should you remain part of that organization?

The reason why countries want to join the Open Government Partnership is not just because they want to say, "we're transparent and we're democracies." The reason is also because it's a group of countries that are successful. In some ways, it is an experiment as well. We are saying these principles are good for our societies; we can succeed as democracies by adhering to them. If you don't adhere to them, you hurt yourself. If you hope to gain prestige by being part of this group and yet are criticized for claiming to have those values that you don't really have, you turn yourself into an object of ridicule. Instead of getting the respect of a country that values transparency and engagement with citizens and of showing itself to be a good democracy, the country becomes an example that others point to as a country that is doing it wrong. We all hold each other up as models.

You spent some eighteen months in Hungary. Would you say that you experienced open government there?

I am not going to speak directly about internal affairs within Hungary. There is an active civil society there. There is a recorded commitment to open government by the government, which is a member of the Open Government Partnership and which is a member of organizations that promote democratic principles, and there are countries that are more closed and authoritarian than Hungary.

Would you name some?

There are. [Laughing.] Citizens have a responsibility, too, especially in a democracy. We are getting back to what we talked about with regards to the type of society in Hungary and the nature of people, of citizens. They are very educated, very friendly, willing to talk, but also not confident about their own ability to affect things. They could speak with more confidence, to have that positive attitude that "we shape our society, and we need to work together to do that." Democracy is not just a matter of electing a government and forgetting about it. It's not just a matter of hoping that the government will follow rules; it also means constant engagement between citizens and government. It's a responsibility for citizens to be engaged and to hold the government accountable. This responsibility has to be accepted and there must be concern when this responsibility is not carried out. It is not just "wag their finger" at the government or say that they just can't do it because they're not strong enough or that they don't agree with other people or that they can't work with them. There is a big responsibility for citizens as well in a democracy. Citizens get the government that they take responsibility for.

This is true, especially in the long run.

I can talk about my own government. If a government commits itself to certain ideals and principles, then rather than saying, "yes, yes, they have done it, but they don't really mean it," or "we should ignore what they say," or "that they're all liars and it's just politics," it's better to say, "this is a commitment that the government has made. It's my responsibility to hold them to this commitment. It's my responsibility to know what the commitments are that my government has made, and to hold them accountable." This is, again, one of the principles of open government. The citizens need to know what their government is doing, especially if they agree with the principles, the steps that the government is taking, or the aspirations the government has set; the citizens need to track them and hold the government accountable. The citizens need to register their discontent if the government is not doing what it has committed itself to doing.

There is currently this issue about your former Secretary of State Hilary Clinton's using her private e-mail account for State Department business, which is a violation of proper procedure.

Even there you can see how important the question of being transparent and being accountable is. We are responding to the request of Congress and to public requests to get this information out as quickly as we can. This is information that is being made available in the public interest.

When a country that obviously does not exercise open government joins the open government initiative, wouldn't its participation hurt the credibility of the initiative? Of course, you might hope that becoming a member in the partnership might shift even such a government in the direction of more openness.

Naively or not, I try to take what a person says or a government says at face value. If a government says "these are the things that we are going to do," then I expect that they are making a serious commitment to do that. If a government subscribes to certain values and says, "these are the things that we will do," then that's a positive step right there, but it is the responsibility of the organization to track and see: does the government do what it says it would do, or is it only that it is saying it on paper, but not following through? The United States should be held to account to its National Action Plan as well. That's the commitment we all make by putting our plans on the table, and all those plans are available on-line. We expect our civil society organizations and any person to hold us to account, and to complain, and to highlight if we are not following our plan, and we would expect the organization to review that. You've raised various concerns about the Hungarian government. The OSCE, the Organization for Security and Co-operation in Europe, has released its reports with regards to the 2014 elections in Hungary and it made a number of recommendations there. The OSCE is following what's happening with regards to those recommendations. The European Union is talking now about the adherence to European values. Of course, it has to define what those values are. Being a member of a values-based organization requires that you adhere to the values of that organization. It's important for those organizations to track adherence and to encourage each other to adhere to those values. These values are not to punish ourselves with; we don't subscribe to these values because we want to harm ourselves. We're saying that these are things that are important for our benefit and that these are our aspirations. This is the vision we have for our society and if we are falling back on that then we want others to help us.

For example, if you are living in the neighborhood and everyone in the neighborhood says: "We want this to be a nice neighborhood, we want the houses to look good, we want the people here to behave in a certain way to each other, to follow certain courtesies, and we want our children to be able to play safely in our neighborhood," this may be in an agreement among the members of the neighborhood and everybody in that neighborhood says: "Yes, we agree to this, because this is the kind of neighborhood that we want." If one of your neighbors starts not following those guidelines; starts letting their property fall into disarray; starts letting their dog run loose where it is not supposed to run loose; it's not a matter of interfering in that person's business by saying, "these were the things that we'd agreed to." In many cases, a neighbor would want to be told if they are violating agreed neighborhood policies. One would expect that they would be able to say to you if you start not following the common neighborhood policies. Ultimately, your neighborhood will be a better place, because all are watching out for each other as long as you'd all agreed to those policies.

Earlier you said, "There is a recorded commitment to open government by the government which is a member of the Open Government Partnership and which is a member of organizations that promote democratic principles," and "there are countries that are more closed and authoritarian than Hungary." My additional question is, are those countries also members of this Partnership?

Yes, they are. This is an aspirational group. We all are not starting from the same place. We are not to say that we permit only perfect countries in. Countries that may have started from very opaque and authoritarian states, but have said: "We want to move forward in this direction and here is our plan"—this organization accepts that. Then it monitors and helps countries to move forward and meet their aspirations. Instead of throwing out a country that has not met its aspirations, we are looking at ways to help it, to see how it can move forward. That's where the independent review will help and discussions with its colleagues, the other members of this organization, will help.

We also put ourselves on the line and monitor how we in the US adhere to our commitment, and we call upon others to monitor us and tell us when we don't live up to our commitment. This is what I am doing now. I talk with different NGOs (Non-Governmental Organizations) and ask them, what we can, at the State Department, do better? Are we meeting our commitment to the groups that are interested in what we're doing?

Did I even touch on your question?

Yes, you did. It is true that there is very limited possibility to impact what is happening in a country from the outside. Yet it seems to me an ambivalent approach to take it at face value when a government professes adherence to democratic principle, contrary to prior experience, and then merely hope that it will perhaps adhere to those principles in the future. Such an approach may even lend credibility to a government that professes adherence to democratic principles in words and does the opposite. Such an approach may also diminish the effectiveness of civil society in carrying out its responsibility of holding the government accountable. In other words, pretending on the outside that the government is adhering to democracy and thereby hoping that such pretense might shift the behavior of that government may have questionable value especially because it weakens the effectiveness of the efforts of civil society.

It's not quite that. There is an infrastructure in place, and there are benefits that come to a country that part of a democratic community governed by the rule of law. The benefit is not just having a friendly relationship with the United States and with other democracies. It also highlights that that country is stable. If this is so, it's a good place for investment, a good place for businesses, and a good place for people to visit. The country benefits from being seen as living up to those commitments. A casual tourist may not care so much; the casual tourist may not be aware or even interested in what's happening. But people who are investing, they pay attention; they want to know, is my investment safe? Will laws change in an opaque way and in a very sudden manner that will affect my investment? They will give the benefit of doubt for a while, but businesses expect to be partners with the government and know what legislative changes might affect them. They talk with each other. Ultimately, if a government is acting opaquely, is not consulting with businesses, then investment dries up.

Fighting Corruption

You, as a US diplomat, showed strong interest in the presence of corruption in the activities of Hungarian government officials. Whence this interest? You made the biggest headlines during your eighteen months in Hungary when it became known that the US would not let in six Hungarian government officials because of corruption charges.

It was an action. We showed that we are serious with regards to the need for accountability. Corruption is a challenge for democracy; it is a challenge for the corporate world, for trade as well. We are working with fellow democracies and trade is an aspect of that. We are advocates of fair commerce and the reliability of legislation. A company that is going to make an investment should be able to compete fairly with other companies. In safeguarding free trade, countering corruption is important. We have laws that penalize US companies if they engage in corrupt practices. Through the Foreign Corrupt Practices Act, we penalize US companies if they pay a bribe or engage in other illegal activities in order to gain advantages over their competitors. If a US company is in an environment that promotes and facilitates corrupt activity and other companies are able to gain advantages through corruption that the US company can't engage in, that puts the US company at a disadvantage. We are concerned on the trade aspect that the commercial environment might be unfair or that the US companies can't compete in a fair environment. We would take action against the US company if it were involved in such activity just as we take action against foreign officials that engage in corrupt practices.

It's not only with regards to commerce that corruption is important. We are going back to transparency, to the benefit of transparency to democracy, of having an open government. Citizens should be able to shed light on what their government is doing and know that the government is following the course that the citizens have chosen. If government officials are not acting in accordance with their responsibilities, if they are taking advantage of their position to gain a benefit that is not due them and that shouldn't be coming to them, then that subverts democracy. It is not simply a matter of citizens electing a government and expecting that their government is going to carry out the wishes of the citizens or is going to follow the law. In an environment that facilitates corruption, in an opaque environment where decisions are made in secret or where there is little accountability, then elected officials won't carry out what the citizens ask for, but will carry out the wishes of those who pay them. This subverts the democratic process. This creates a situation where the citizens are not satisfied with their government; they can't rely on their government to carry out good policy. It makes such a government a less reliable partner when working with other governments, because you can't be sure of what's going to influence the policies of that government.

What we're advocating, and, again, what open government does and transparency does, is help create an environment where there is accountability and where the factors that affect a decision are clear and apparent. We can work with confidence with those governments because we can see what's affecting their decisions and they are following the practices that are laid out in their legislation, and that they won't be influenced by hidden factors. The citizens will also be more trusting of their government; there will be less of a chance of civil unrest and protests than under a government which is weakened by the lack of confidence of its citizens.

Corruption is an issue wherever it occurs. What we promote is an environment in which corruption is less able to take place. In this regard, it's not merely corruption that we are against; rather, we are working with governments *towards* something. We act towards an infrastructure that facilitates government accountability, which is what transparency provides. We act towards an environment where there is oversight and where the oversight comes not just from someone who is within the system, but also from independent groups. This is where civil society plays a significant role and where civil society is able to see what's happening in the government and can provide their comments as well.

You indicated that six individuals—Hungarian government officials—were denied entry into the United States because of corruption. This action drew a strong response in Hungary. Conspicuously, however, nothing followed on the part of the government despite its declared zero-tolerance policy with regards to corruption. What did this inaction tell you?

It told us exactly what you just said; nothing was done. On the other hand, the actions taken by the United States stand. This was the action that we were able to take. If you look at the Open Government National Action Plan—there were different agency plans, the Department of Justice had a plan, the State Department had a plan, et cetera—one of the initiatives in the National Plan is to use the visa processes, the Presidential Proclamation 7750, more aggressively in countering corruption. This is an approach that is identified in the National Action Plan of 2013 to use as one among the tools that are available to promote transparency, to promote accountability. Our visa process is one of those tools.

It turned out to be quite a powerful tool judging by the reactions it generated. The question remains, what should it tell us that the Hungarian government did not take any action?

We took the action we needed to take; the US took the action the US needed to take. At the time, the Hungarian government was asking that the US provide more information so that it could take action. The issue is not that it's up to the United States to tell another country how to carry out its own laws; it's up to that country to see whether it has a sufficient system of accountability. Is it transparent? These things were not done in secret. It was not a secret conversation that we are releasing now, and what you are asking about now; all of this was a very, very public discussion. The question remains, what do Hungary's citizens expect of their government? One thing that this did lead to was a very big discussion within Hungary with regards to accountability, with regards to the level of corruption within the society. There was a very strong focus on it, and it has remained as an undercurrent. Other issues have shifted the conversations and changed attention, but the discussion about corruption and accountability still needs to be had between the citizens of Hungary and their government.

Can we interpret the lack of follow-up action on the part of official Hungary as a violation of its own principle of zero-tolerance with respect to corruption?

That's something you should be asking Hungarian citizens. I don't want to interpret the government of Hungary's responsiveness with regards to this issue as a foreign observer. If you asked the United States in that regard, do we hold our officials accountable? Do we act upon our commitments to open government?

So I am asking that.

The US does hold its officials accountable. Every year, there is a document that the Department of Justice provides to the Congress with regards to American government officials at the Federal level and at the State level that have been convicted of corruption. It's an open document and it identifies what they've done, who they are. This document provides some level of confidence that we hold our officials to a certain standard. At various times, Americans see their public officials on trial. They will see that even leaders of a State, a governor, can be held for corruption. The former governor of Virginia (Robert McDonnell) was recently convicted of corruption. Of course, this must be handled in court, and if we trust our court system, it cannot just be a revenge of political adversaries.

In Hungary, there have been accusations of political adversaries, and on some occasions, people spent years in jail or under the cloud of such accusations before, at least in some cases, they had to be exonerated.

This is something, again, that citizens of a country need to ask themselves, are we seeing our legislative processes act in the way they should? Are we seeing our officials held accountable? It should not just be a matter of accusations made in the media, but of an actual criminal process leading to a conviction or leading to the person not being convicted. The process should be an open one where the charges are made and the evidence is presented. That is something the country should look at, look at the region, have those due trials take place. Corruption is around in other countries too, and at varying degrees, but it is not a question of the level of corruption; it is a question of accountability.

You identified six high-level Hungarian government officials, high-level, but not the highest-level officials, and decided that they would not be let into the United States because of corruption. One wonders inevitably if you have only six such persons and only at the level of the hierarchy where these officials are. One tends to suppose that you may have information about a larger number of government officials and including higher-level government figures, and that the six singled out is just a sample, creating a test case to see what happens. What was the consideration?

The consideration was .... at a particular time, what evidence do we have that we consider reliable and what does that evidence lead to?

The reaction to this action was considerable within the society if not in government actions. Your action stirred up the political scenery in Hungary. Could this be considered a warning?

It can be considered that the US does have tools in place to take action with regards to corruption. As we state in our Open Government National Action Plan, this is a tool that we should use with the appropriate effect. This is what was done.

Protecting Civil Society

You have paid particular attention to the role of civil society.

In discussing the situation in Hungary, I am referring to the period particularly a year ago [2014], when the actions against civil society were taking place. This was an issue raised by the President with respect to the crackdown of civil society.

President Obama.

President Obama in September 2014—it was at the end of a year in which civil society had been a focus of his administration. There was a "Stand with Civil Society" initiative. Over the course of this year, we were looking for ways to provide more support for civil society. This was not just to support individual initiatives, but to create an environment in which civil society is able to thrive, where it plays its role as a valuable partner to government, and furthers the cause of good governance. At the end of this year of "Stand with Civil Society," speaking at the Clinton Global Initiative, on the eve of his UN speech, President Obama laid out the importance of civil society within a democratic country. Many of the innovations that helped society move forward come not from within government itself, but from private sector and from civil society. This includes furthering the cause of civil rights, human rights, and supporting oppressed minority groups. In creating a better society, the ideas often don't come from the government itself, but come from engagement of civil society.

During that speech on September 23, 2014, President Obama also noted areas and countries where civil society was under threat, where workers in civil society organizations and non-governmental organizations (NGOs) were imprisoned. He mentioned places, countries, where civil organizations were targeted by those who opposed their activities or where the civil organizations were being made the targets of excessive bureaucracy. He mentioned different countries within his speech and one of the countries he mentioned was Hungary. His exact words were, citing the entire paragraph, so as not to take his words out of context, as follows, "From Russia to China to Venezuela, you are seeing relentless crackdowns, vilifying legitimate dissent as subversive. In places like Azerbaijan, laws make it incredibly difficult for NGOs even to operate. From Hungary to Egypt, endless regulations and overt intimidation increasingly target civil society. And around the world, brave men and women who dare raise their voices are harassed and attacked and even killed."[11]

As Hungary was mentioned in the same sentence with Egypt, it drew a strong reaction from the Hungarian government. There was a question as to whether civil society is in fact under threat in Hungary. This was something that I was asked about. Given that there had been police raids on civil society organizations, that several of the tax numbers were being suspended, that there was this audit taking place by the Hungarian government, it was hard to deny that there were steps taken against independent civil society organizations. This was something that was mentioned twice within the OSCE, the first time in June 2014, shortly after the audits were launched and the US made a statement within the OSCE. Later on, there was a second statement after police raids following the special report on the media by Dunja Mijatovic, the OSCE Representative on Freedom of the Media. She also cited the same concerns with regards to civil society and freedom of media in Hungary.

The concerns were expressed with regards to civil society. We were working together with other countries within the OSCE as a community of like-minded nations, democratic nations, to highlight the importance of civil society to a strong democracy. We were not trying to give undue criticism, but to explain how we see our societies. What is the nature of our democracy? What are the things that we should watch against if we want to preserve our democracy as one that's responsive to the needs of its citizens, as countries that are able to work as effective partners with other democracies? Accountability, transparency, strong civil society—those are all factors and elements of open government.

---

11 Remarks by the President at Clinton Global Initiative, Para. 17, Obama White House Archives, September 23, 2014, https://obamawhitehouse.archives.gov/the-press-office/2014/09/23/remarks-president-clinton-global-initiative.

Stability versus Instability

In science we sometimes deal with a so-called metastable state, which is, for example, an oversaturated solution, a salt solution in which there is more salt dissolved than what can be had in solution under normal circumstances. Although the solution continues to exist, and shows no sign of problems externally, it is not in a stable state. Having this instability, upon throwing another piece of salt, however small, into the system, suddenly there is precipitation. To me, authoritarian and totalitarian regimes appear like oversaturated solutions of instability. Seemingly, everything is quiet, but then a little disturbance happens and the regime collapses. It may take a long time before this happens, but then something may bring it down and very quickly, overnight. Authoritarian and totalitarian states are unstable and this instability will contribute to their demise. Democracies are more stable in spite of their often disorderly appearance. I'm sure the analogy is not perfect, but it may hint that we may witness some interesting events, sooner or later. Of course, when I am referring to an overnight collapse, it may not be taken literally but it may be "overnight" on a historical scale. The collapse of the Soviet Union had been predicted from the time of its formation. However, when it finally did happen, even the most celebrated Kremlinologists were taken by surprise. One of the little grains of salt that fatally disturbed the Soviet regime was when a handful of powerless Soviet citizens declared that they wanted to emigrate.

I've thought about this in a different context, about the advantages and disadvantages of authoritarian and totalitarian systems, for example, the communist economic system versus the capitalist free market, or authoritarian versus democratic systems. The centralized control within an authoritarian system requires intense effort. Perhaps, this is a type of system, using different analogies, which is more geared to the Industrial Age. In an Industrial Age environmental hierarchy is easier to enforce, where you have limited channels of information, where a person at the top is able to send orders down through a chain of command that has to be adhered to, and where information comes up through the same chain of command. There is no other source of information than what's going through those limited channels. There is no other way for people to interact with each other; in that type of limited information environment, a hierarchical system is able to thrive and able to exercise central control. Democratic systems, systems where people are able to exercise their own will, are able to govern themselves, they can be self-governing and self-organizing as well; however, this is very difficult on a large scale.

We, in the US, have a loose system of self-organizing entities; we have the Federal level, but much of the governing is taking place at the state and local levels. We don't have directives that go straight from the top and that are implemented very quickly at the local level. Our government is geared towards carrying out much of its politics locally. If something collapses in one town, it doesn't necessarily affect the next town. The infrastructure is very loose, and now we come to the analogy: A small rupture at one place can be corrected easily and it does not affect the entire infrastructure. In a more hierarchical system, that local rupture could affect the whole structure. The inability of the center to convey orders to the bottom, or the inability of information to flow back to the top, paralyzes the structure under centralized control.

In modern times, the information systems have improved, the structures have changed the people's ability to access information no matter where they are. People at the top can reach directly to the bottom, and the information flow can also happen from the bottom to the top, bypassing the hierarchical structure. This makes it possible to organize laterally, or jump up two levels, or correspond with others two or three levels away. This has changed the hierarchical system. This has changed how societies are organized. It has also helped lead to a breakdown within hierarchical organizations as people disregard the hierarchy, or as the center tries to enforce a hierarchy that can no longer be enforced. This could lead to paralysis within the system; it could lead to false information being passed up to the top, because people are afraid of micromanagement. These are some of the aspects that have led to breakdowns of authoritarian systems. Where there is information coming from uncontrolled sources and people are able to interact with it and with each other, they will no longer respect the hierarchy.

Within collaborative, democratic societies, the challenge is different. There is still some type of hierarchical structure, but the challenge is to work with the abundance of information we now have and to work with transparency. We can't control information in the same way that we used to. If our citizens don't find something out from us, they find it out from some other place. If they don't trust their government, they don't work with their government. Because of our ability to communicate globally, it is no longer the case that small, local government organizations are disconnected, without a regional impact. There are interest groups that communicate beyond the visible borders. There are entities now that cross the state lines. They can organize effectively and very quickly. They have the information they need to mobilize citizens. Here is where that crystallizing effect occurs that you were talking about. You drop in a seed. Whereas, prior to the existence of these technologies, it was possible to localize the effect, now it spreads very, very quickly throughout a very, very large system. If you have a leadership which is not able to engage with its public effectively, which is not able to have the conversations with them that it needs to have, which is out of touch, which had locked itself up in an ivory tower—using the old expression—then it does not know that change is taking place, and it is taking place much more rapidly than it used to take place. That leadership can find that the environment has changed overnight, and the leadership does not have the ability to respond. Things become chaotic.

With the approach that we are talking about: open government; transparency; engagement with citizens; valuing the role of civil society, we have an ongoing network where people are getting their information not from just one or two sources, but they're getting it from numerous sources, including from their own government. In this type of system, if you are not providing information, then you're excluded from the discussion. Using a different example from the world of science, if scientists are making fantastic discoveries, but not providing their papers for peer review or not engaging in the discussion with the community, then, regardless how beneficial their information might be, such scientists are not part of the overall discussion. Things may change for better or worse, they will find that they have no impact on the scientific environment if they are not contributing their information to the discussion.

With transparency, with openness, government is contributing to the public discussion much more effectively, helping to shape that discussion. With the engagement of citizens, it remains part of the change or is managing the change. There is no change to the system that will happen without some type of government awareness or government engagement. If the government is seen as a credible partner, then people will also rely on their government to help them get through these changes.

I am bringing back the example of my experience when working with American citizens in Syria. We engaged them throughout a crisis process where things were happening around them very quickly. We were part of the discussion, so that the situation our citizens found themselves in wouldn't change too quickly without us being aware and trying to assist. This constant engagement is not just beneficial within a crisis environment. We did the same thing when I was in London. We made an extra effort to engage with our American citizens in Britain through many different channels, because many did feel a need to engage with us.

I'll now compare Britain with Syria. In Syria, it was easy for us to engage with American citizens, because they relied on us very heavily. They wanted to be sure that their embassy knew that they were there, because there was always the prospect of trouble. They wanted to work with us. In Britain, an English-speaking country, our citizens didn't have to relate to their embassy at all. They could just go to their embassy when they were in trouble. At other times, it was as if their embassy did not exist. We wanted to be part of the discussion. We wanted to be engaged with the community of American citizens there during normal times and not be just an afterthought when there was a problem. You never know what's going to happen in an environment.

While I was in Britain, there was a terrorist attack in 2005 on the transportation system. There were tornados, surprisingly. We had a system in place where we could reach out to people in affected areas, and we reached out to them before crises happened. They knew that we were there, that we cared about our citizens, and we were not just waiting for them to contact us during an emergency. In the current circumstance, transparency combined with engagement helps lead to a situation where the government is not caught off guard by changes within the society. Citizens see themselves as partners with their government. They want to work with their government as it advances through changes in society, cultural changes and changes in technology.

Education and Economy

*Let's talk a little about education. However puzzling the concept of illiberal democracy is, it has been claimed that authoritarian regimes in Southeastern Asia are doing very well by paying a lot of attention to the quality of education, and there is, indeed, economic success. What do you think of such a combination? Before we move to this topic, I do not think the current Hungarian model follows this Southeast Asian model because what we are witnessing is the combination of an authoritarian regime with diminishing attention to the **quality** of education.*

We are proponents of free market and competition. When I mention free market, I don't mean an anarchic or a chaotic market, but a free market with a certain amount of regulation. I mean a free market where competition is promoted. There are guidelines, but the economy is not so strictly controlled that companies don't have an incentive to compete. In contrast, a rigid structure may look efficient at the outset, but it's not flexible; it can't change with the changing economy. It becomes like the five-year plans.

The United States has very strong economic ties with China. Politically, China is very rigid; there is some inherent instability in its huge economy that may be ascribable to the rigidity of its overall system. My question is whether this instability might influence the United States in case of unexpected change in China and whether the flexibility of the United States would suffice to fend off any negative consequences of unwelcome changes in the Chinese economy. A few weeks ago, this might have been more of an academic question whereas, in light of the recent sudden devaluation of the Chinese currency and the quick reaction to it in the US stock market, this has demonstrated that this may be a more practical question than we might have thought before.

Of course, this is a different question from the earlier one that was about the efficiency of these controlled economic systems, which highlights the weaknesses in these controlled systems. The smaller economies may be manageable, but it's hard to continue with such a controlled system in a changing economic environment with a small number of people making the decisions all the time to keep the economy going in the right direction. I am not an economist and I'm not able to talk with any kind of expertise there about what's happening now. The easy answer to your question about whether the instability of the Chinese system would affect the United States and the world is that it is such a large economy, which has invested around the world, and which is also a market for world goods that, of course, it has an impact. Vice versa, changes in the US economy also impact the Chinese economy as they do the world economy. The question is which one will endure over the long term: which type of system; the one, which promotes greater flexibility, self-correction and innovation in how it deals with tremors in the marketplace, or the one where there is a bureaucratic process in place to centrally manage the direction of the economy? Other countries are looking at these systems and trying to choose the one that suits them.

We have diverted from the question of education and I am suggesting we return to it. The current Hungarian government promotes less demanding and more regimented education. For this direction, the model tacitly or overtly is the political system that operated between the two world wars.

Why the simplification of education? And, why is the model of the Horthy era attractive? To speculate about this, one would have to accept that the present political system is modeling itself after the Horthy era.

Didn't you see signs of this?

I heard people talking about it, but I am not enough of an expert on educational systems to make an informed comparison between the educational systems of the Horthy era and the one developing under the present conditions.

Have you formed an impression about the similarity of the political philosophies between the Horthy era and the current regime?

I don't want to make specific comparisons between the political philosophies of a past era and the current one. There will have to be some significant differences, if only because they are two different eras. Rather than making a comparison with another era, let's simply talk about the current trends in education and about the current trends in political philosophy—and what kind of things those lead to. What is taught in schools, the school curriculum, is very important with regard to shaping the direction of society over a generation, having an impact on schoolchildren and how they understand the society around them. Whether in elementary school or more advanced levels, in high school, and in university, in each stage, shaping that child's or that young adult's perspective of history, of society, of cultural values, is very important for a government, for a society. What is in the curriculum? What is our vision of ourselves? What is our vision of our society, and how do we want to think of our society in the future? What the teachers are teaching the children now will determine what the children will think of society in the future.

In the United States, we have focused a lot on the nature of education, what it says about civic engagement: how well do our children and our high school students understand their responsibilities as citizens within a democracy? There are huge debates within the United States about the cultural elements that are within the educational system, whether it is with regard to the role of religion, or with regard to the cultural values inherent in science, or whether the children should be taught negative things about their country, or whether they should only be taught positive things about their country.

The educational system, including the curriculum, does not have a centrally directed character in the United States.

There is more of a drive towards that, but we don't have it yet.

When you say "yet," you think there will be?

There is always discussion. The United States is comprised of fifty states and the fifty states generally govern their own educational systems. Each of those states has school districts, and we've tended to leave the curriculum to the district to determine its agenda, with state input. There's been more centralization of what should be in that curriculum to try to make sure that there is not a big disparity between the districts and that all students would be able to be competitive for university. There are still debates about what should be included in the curriculum and whether students are expected to study only what is going to be on a test. This is as opposed to being able to think more broadly than just what will be on a test, and to study things that would be useful for them in the furthering of their development and critical thinking, even if it is not going to be something that they are tested on: imbuing them with an intellectual curiosity where they question the society around them and ask their teachers questions. We often expect our students to ask questions of their teachers and think beyond what they're being taught. This is a comparison that I've heard between the US system and the Hungarian system. When I would speak with students, they would often talk about the Prussian system of education. This is how the Hungarian students described it; it was the first time I heard it described that way. In that system, the students are not expected to ask questions of the teacher. The Prussian system places the teacher as the authority.

Looking Back

Hungary fought against the United States in World War II, and more than that, Hungary declared war against the United States immediately after Germany and the US had become belligerent parties in 1941. The United States was not in a hurry to consider itself at war with Hungary and closed its embassy in Budapest only about half a year later. We used to talk about the liberation of Hungary in 1945, but this is no longer the case, at least, for many. Hungary and the US are now allies and both are members of NATO. However, from time to time, you can sense uneasiness on the part of official Hungary and this uneasiness is about how to handle Hungary's history in World War II. It seems as if Germany has solved its problem more unambiguously. I am asking you if you have experienced any sentiments—either way—about the Hungarian-American relationship of today or in historical context. I can give you a piece of experience I had in the US. A few years ago, soon after my biography of Edward Teller had come out, I had been asked to give a talk about him in the Hungarian Library in New York. The talk was well attended and the atmosphere was friendly. However, before the talk, in front of the building, as the organizers and I were being photographed, a lady confronted me saying, "how could I write a book about a traitor of Hungary who prepared a devastating bomb for his fatherland's mortal enemy." She did not wait for me to respond, turned, and left. She did not come to the talk. As it turned out some people knew her and told me she was an American citizen.

Americans like Hungary. They didn't want to fight a war with Hungary. Even after the United States had already been at war with Germany, the US did not immediately declare war with Hungary, even though Hungary was an ally of Germany. The sense some people conveyed to me in Hungary was that Hungary was a victim of Germany—this seems to be the current sentiment. People told me that Hungary was an unwilling ally of Germany. More people expressed their concern to me about the American role in 1956 than about the state of war between us in World War II. If anything, they tried to make it clear that, in spite of the alliance with Germany, Hungarians still favored the US and would have liked to have been liberated by the Americans. Whether it's a myth or not, people would convey that Hungarians died tragically during World War II, that it was victimized by Germany, it tried to leave, but was forced to be part of this war, so what could it do? No hard feelings. Of course, this was so, except for the places where America bombed. Some people would come to me and say that it would be nice for America to make some gesture of understanding with regards to towns in Hungary that had been bombed by American aircraft, an acknowledgment of the damage that had been done. Of course, we all do regret the damage of war and World War II was a terrible war, but we were fighting for the right thing. It is an important question, how this is reflected in Hungarian textbooks, Hungary's role in World War II, and what *it* was fighting for—because Hungarian soldiers were fighting—and Hungary was not fighting on the side of the right. The foot soldiers were following orders, but at a certain level, you can't deny responsibility. Countries have to deal with this question. Germany had to deal with it, as did Austria. We are happy to say what our soldiers were fighting for.

The whole approach to history and the history of our relations shows that we have a strong history and we have to deal with it, and Hungary has to deal with it: What were its soldiers fighting for? This was something that I used to discuss when I was in Hungary. It is not something that began recently. Our relationship with Hungary goes back to the beginnings of our own nation and the United States' struggle for freedom. This was when we were laying out our principles of unalienable human rights of freedom from an empire, freedom from a monarchy, freedom of people governing and taking responsibility for themselves as citizens and shaping their own society. This inspired a number of Hungarians to join us in that fight. One of them was a Colonel Kováts who joined us. In his letter to Benjamin Franklin, he made it very clear that he was doing this as a matter of principle, because he is Hungarian, and he loves freedom. This guided him towards joining our struggle and helping us create a cavalry, and he died in fighting for American freedom. That was in the 1700s. With these shared principles and shared values, changing over time, what freedom and liberty might have meant in the eighteenth century was different in the nineteenth century and they are different in the twenty-first century. In the nineteenth century, Hungarians were fighting for liberty as well and for the establishment of their independent state. This was something that the United States tacitly supported to the anger of the Austrians. The level of our support was something that only came out afterwards.

We were a strong supporter of the various freedom movements in the nineteenth century and in this desire for constitutional states with citizens being able to guide their own destiny. We had a lot of immigration between our countries in the nineteenth century. There was the establishment of consulates, and Hungarians, Austrians and others from the Carpathian basin came to the United States, sharing their values and helping to shape American society. Some of them then returned to Hungary with values that helped shape Hungarian society. We in the US were entering the diplomatic world as a great power, entering diplomatic relations; we had to accommodate our perspectives in some ways to the formalities of international diplomacy at the end of the nineteenth century. Hungary was very much in that world now, being part of a monarchy; there was stratification of society but also engagement by the citizens.

Citizens were not very much engaged, and Hungary did not have an independent foreign policy.

But it did have citizens who, in the late nineteenth century, were engaged in building a capital that they could be proud of.

That was very much so. It was a very progressive era in building a modern infrastructure.

The source of that progress was not government initiative necessarily, but people and their support of local society. There was more stratification during this period, with different levels of society and the nobility.

After World War I, the US perspective on nationalism influenced the European perspective on nationalism and the creation of nation-states. There is still a lot of ongoing discussion in Hungarian society about whether these states based upon ethnicity should have been created or whether the multicultural—with all the vagueness of this concept—nature of the Austro-Hungarian Empire should have been maintained. Strengthened national identities developed with ethnic nation-states and Hungary felt victimized by having lost territory, especially in which Hungarian ethnic groups resided. The desire to gain back lost territories impacted so many of Hungary's decisions, leading to the side it allied with in World War II, where, once again, we were on the opposite sides of the fence. However, the core love of freedom and the sense of individualism and the desire to be able to shape one's own society, that connected us as people, remained. What divided us was the difference in governance. Then, after just a few brief years of exercising some form of democracy, Hungary came under communism, and this shaped our nations' perspectives even more. People in Hungary now remember the hope that America offered in the 1950s to free them from communism. During World War II, Hungarians wished that the Americans had liberated them; but, they were liberated by the Soviets. Now, in the 1950s, people were looking towards America to help them, and a feeling of betrayal developed, whether betrayal at Yalta or betrayal in 1956. The Hungarians' sense that the US was not there when they needed us; I don't believe that this perspective is entirely accurate, but it is the sentiment that people conveyed to me.

Could we learn more about your conversations with Hungarians while you were in Hungary about Yalta and especially about the expectations and disappointments in Hungary of American actions in and immediately after 1956?

There are Hungarians who feel betrayed because they believe that the United States let the country fall under the Soviet sphere of interest in the 1945 Yalta agreement and that the US did not take action to help the Hungarian freedom fighters in 1956. I would not say that the US "betrayed" Hungary in 1956. What I would say about these two events is that the US stands for the same values that Hungarians have stood for, and this has been valid throughout our joint history. Like in 1989, the United States did not come and "liberate" Hungary. Fighting for one's principles and knowing that one has an ally with regard to these shared principles is something that that the US has tried hard to convey. Ultimately, however, democracy is a matter of self-governance; democracy is not being imposed by another power, but by people being able to express themselves. We highlighted that Hungarians live up to their principles even under the most difficult conditions. In 1956, we were not there to push the Soviets out.

There were misleading programs in the Western media, American media, broadcast to Hungary that could have been interpreted as if only the Hungarians would hold out long enough—presidential elections were coming up in just a few days—there might be intervention. Realistically, there could have not been intervention, but we are not discussing now what was and what was not realistic; only, how people could have perceived what they thought they were learning from these broadcasts.

Let's turn the issue around. If Radio Free Europe or other media had not encouraged Hungarians to hold out; rather, if they would have told the Hungarians: "Behave yourselves; don't fight; you have no chance; stop!" That might have also generated a feeling of abandonment - and worse, that the US no longer supported the principle that citizens should stand up for what they believe in. It's hard to know what was expected. This relates to one of the central topics of our conversation, citizen engagement. We have always encouraged democracy, the establishment of democracy. Now we are doing this via the Open Government partnership program. In 1956, people were expecting that there would be some type of military support.

The problem was not just that they were expecting, but that they were led to expect it; at least this was the perception. It did not happen, and it could not have happened, but the perception was there and inevitable disappointment followed.

Let's shift to now and examine how government and people communicate now. In 1956, people were listening to short-wave radios. They picked up what they could, what Western governments were saying, and then information propagated from person to person. There was no real conversation and there was no such engagement of the type that's possible now. The ability to communicate and to engage has developed enormously. There are also more challenges today than before. Government still participates in part of the engagement, but there is also real-time, person-to-person communication, NGO-to-NGO communication, taking place all the time. I just heard on the radio on my way here about the Pope and his use of Twitter. It's giving the people a sense that here is a person that they can engage with. This technology is humanizing this person that used to be far away who has enormous authority. He still has enormous authority, but now he has the ability to humanize his authority and engage to such an extent that had never been possible.

I'm glad you distinguished between what happened in reality and what those sentiments are. When people have sentiments that romanticize reality that is excusable. However, the Hungarian government is feeding those sentiments with falsification of history. Just to mention the blatant recent example of the infamous new memorial on Szabadság tér, which in essence officially proclaims Hungary an innocent victim of Nazi Germany.

Moving forward, after 1956 to some extent—1956 is eclipsed by America standing strong against the Soviet Union, against communism, leading to the regime changes in 1989 and the fall of the Iron Curtain. We were always there, supporting the desire for freedom, but people don't always succeed in their desire, and there is only a certain amount that foreign countries can do at different points. At the end, in 1989, Hungary became a success story with its transition to democratic government, to quickly move to looking like it always had similar values: the love of freedom, the love of shaping its own society, and engaging with society. That there was actual discussion at the round table (Ellenzéki Kerekasztal) and a reasoned approach to move towards democracy highlights this ability to integrate effectively into an environment where democratic perspectives and a way to compromise and work with those different perspectives are valued. Hungary was an excellent candidate for integrating well into the Western European society. This is not just a matter of democratic principle, but also maintaining it as a republican principle—in this case, republican meaning that it's not just the pure majority that determines the shape of the country, but also the rule of law and the protection of minorities from the dictatorship of the majority. This is the recognition of the need, together, in a legal framework that protects the rights that people fought for. That's where we work together to hold ourselves to our aspirations.

We in the US see ourselves as a democratic country with aspirations of treating everyone equally and safeguarding our human and civil rights. We receive criticism for occasionally falling down on those efforts. For example, you mentioned in your writings, how you didn't even realize that you should've been dismayed by what happened at Kent State, at the time when it happened, but you realized later, what happened at Kent State was a poor example of the United States' respect of freedom of speech.

We took criticism for that; we take criticism; we acknowledge criticism for what are seen as our civil rights failures in the 1960s. We criticize ourselves and we accept criticism for what's happening with discrimination with different ethnic groups, racism in the United States, with police actions in some cases where there has been death caused by what has appeared to be police abuse. We accept the criticism that these things do not live up to the type of ideals we hold. We try to address them. Look at what it's brought about: the discussion of holding people accountable. We have a window now on what's happening through smart phones and people taking videos of incidents, which directly contradict official statements. The question is what would've happened without this window, compared to what really happened? What would've happened if there was no other evidence, if there was no information other than the official response? Would people have been held accountable?

Transparency leads to accountability. Just this week, I was reading about more and more cities that are requiring police to wear cameras on their clothes so that there will always be some video evidence of what is taking place. This makes it harder to do something that is in secret for which you will not be held accountable. This is where we accept our mistakes and we take criticism, and we look to change our behavior, and hold ourselves accountable through transparency, through engaging civil society, which also will hold us up to the light and say, we expect you to do better.

I just spent half an hour talking about this long history and why we expect our government to do better. We will listen to our citizens and to the criticism of other countries, and we hope that we can be a good example. We also, therefore, see it as appropriate and natural that we would talk with those other countries in the same way. We all need the comments of our friends, of those who believe, like us, who share the same values, to make sure that we live up to our aspirations. This is really what this whole discussion is about, with every country that we can be partners with. We can say we have shared values. I just spent quite some time talking about the development of shared values with Hungary. This is not something that happens overnight and can therefore be wiped out overnight as well. It's not that we have huge differences in cultural values. Over two hundred years, we have grown together and we believe in very similar things, in things that we subscribe to. The nature of what we want our societies to be is also what we expect our friends to keep us true to.

About the monument on Szabadság tér, do you care to comment?

The government missed an opportunity to engage civil society—to have a meaningful discussion about historical events of enormous importance.

There was not even an unveiling of the monument. Had there been an unveiling, would you have attended it if invited?

I doubt it. Of course, you're referring to a hypothetical situation. As we said in our statement when they began to erect that monument, this is an opportunity for discussion. An issue of this magnitude requires that there be an engagement between citizens and government. In this case, there wasn't one. That discussion did not take place. In contrast, the living memorial (Eleven Emlékmű) across the street was a fascinating exercise—the lifeless monument and the living monument to which people were coming very regularly in large numbers to discuss the history of the period. They raised questions, gave their accounts, turned those stones into a gathering place for people to hear different perspectives and to see the different artifacts that people laid out there. The story became very different from that which the government had intended to present. I regularly heard tour groups going to that area and heard the tour guide stopping and explaining not just about the monument, but about everything else they were seeing there. The foreigners who came to that spot got a much better understanding of the complex debate taking place in Hungary and were often more sympathetic to those who had laid the mementos than they would have been if the monument had not been there in the first place and the stories had not come out this way.

In ten or twenty years, or even much sooner, the tour groups will see the monument only and the alternative exhibition will have faded in oblivion.

If we look back, say, forty years, at the monuments that existed in Hungary, who would have predicted what would happen to some of those monuments? Stones are not permanent. If there is discussion, if history is not forgotten and people make an effort not to forget history, and to convey it to their children– if the stones are still there and if they still attract attention at all, either people will be passing by and not think about them, or their understanding will be colored by what society will think about them at the time. I learned from the books you'd written that many monuments are not noticed and people don't know what they mean. We don't know what the shape of Hungarian society—or US society—will be in fifteen or twenty-five years.

Communication and Politics

Let's talk a little more about modern means of communication and open government.

The changes in modern communication techniques had made it easier for us to speak about government being open, but, of course, the concept is not new. The idea that in a democracy you need to engage the citizens because they are the core of democracy has been one of the basic premises of the American form of democracy since the beginning. The liberal nature of democracy was in contrast to the very structured hierarchical systems where the authority was not seen as coming from citizens, but from other sources; it was a foreordained structure in which people were predestined to rule, because they were given that authority by right of birth or by divine power.

Has the relationship of American politics to the term liberal undergone some change? When I visited the US for the first time, in 1969, many considered it something dirty or even intent to undermine American democracy whereas my impression today is that it has become more accepted by the mainstream.

It depends on whom you are talking to. You are right that there have been periods in the history of the United States when the term *liberal* was synonymous with progressive or someone who believes that the role of government is to take care of people. You cannot be hard; you should not take the tough line, and you should always have a softer, humanitarian approach. Liberals were seen as more aligned with those who favored peace. They were the doves in the discussions in the 1960s and the hawks were those who favored using force and looking just at the pragmatic aspects of the situation; more of the Machiavellian types. The term *liberal* was often paired with the expression "bleeding heart" liberals; their hearts were always bleeding for other people, and they were not looking at things in a pragmatic way in order to get problems resolved. That was the formulation in that period when you were here for your first visit to the US in the 1960s.

If we go back to how the term *liberal* was used when it was first used in a political sense in the 1700s it was meant to signify being free, to be a free person. It meant that people are the source of power in a government, that the authority to govern comes from the people; that it is not coming from a right to govern, that there are no natural hierarchies, or subjects who are not free and who have to respect the preordained order. Liberalism is a system in which there are human rights and the government is there by the consent of the governed in order to safeguard those rights. Citizens are essential in determining the nature of their government. The citizens need to be engaged.

This type of thinking is found in the American *Declaration of Independence*. We formed a government based upon the consent of the citizens; and the right of the government comes from that consent. In that formulation, in that basic idea of a liberal democratic system where citizens are the source of a government's authority, there has to be communication. The government has to open itself up, has to communicate with its citizens. A government operating in secrecy conflicts with the idea of citizens being able to determine the course of their government. Citizens have to know what is going on. From the beginning of our republic, the United States, we've highlighted the importance of education, of having an informed, educated electorate to be able to exercise its rights as citizens in an informed way. This is the importance of a good school system, of education within society, so that citizens play their role and take on their responsibility in determining the course of their government. This is not something new. It has always been recognized that, in a democracy, there has to be some type of communication between government and the governed or that there should be freedom of information. This has been a theme of open government from the very beginning. Exercising it though, finding ways to enable government to be open, has been challenging.

Going back two centuries, how could you share information? What were the ways in which people could understand what was happening in their government? If you are not physically located in the same place, if you could not travel to the place where the records were kept, it might be hard to see what your government was doing. The farther away things were, the less you had direct access to them. This is how it has developed that we must rely on our representatives. This is why we elect people that we trust to represent us in the halls of government, and they are responsible to us. We elect them to represent us based upon their judgment, but they are still responsible to those who elect them.

Now, we are coming to an age where we don't have to be physically in the same place in order to have access to information. Communication technologies have developed from telegraphs and newspapers, to film and telephone, to radio and television, and now the Internet in this digital age of telecommunication. It is now possible for governments to make their information accessible, and not just make it accessible to the public in a one-way flow of information, but for the public to be able to express its opinions and its concerns, directly to the government in an open way using these tools.

You said that one of the reasons to elect representatives was to overcome the difficulties of access to records, to information, in general. Is the reverse also true that by progress in telecommunication, we will see the form of government through representatives becoming obsolete?

I think it is changing and I don't know it will ever be obsolete. People now have direct access to medical information and people can read these online materials and check themselves to see whether or not they are sick. They can diagnose themselves, but does that mean that we won't need doctors? Just because all the information that doctors were expected to be expert in is available to the public, doesn't mean that people don't need to turn to someone whose primary focus is going to be as an expert in those matters. The same applies to almost anything whether it is to fix your car, to put together a television program; it doesn't mean that people now no longer need to have someone whose role it is to provide specialized expertise—including representatives whose expertise is governance.

So we'll always need politicians?

What there may be is more of an expectation that the representative will be more in direct communication with those who have elected him or her.

Is it a changing function?

The relationship is changing. These people are still there to understand the concerns of the citizens who elected them and to represent those concerns in government. It is also their function to make their decisions based upon their expertise.

Would it be step forward in this development to organize more frequent referenda, like the Swiss do about the most diverse issues?

It wouldn't necessarily be a step forward; it would be a different form of the democratic system. We have a representative system, but we have the possibility of direct ballots and a number of states in the United States do have referenda whereby the citizens of that state are able to draft legislation. They have a referendum and have the citizens vote on that legislation. It then becomes state law because the citizens had voted on it. Within the United States, each state has its own system. Some allow this type of referendum, other states don't; but that's not a step forward, it's just a different way to implement democracy.

Modern technology makes exercising such a form of democracy easier.

Modern technology is available, but it is still the decision of the citizens working together with government to see whether this is how they want to govern themselves and govern their state. The question can arise, do we elect people to represent us and to use their expertise to base their decisions not simply on what the majority of voters would like to have, but also to use their judgment and understanding of the constitution and laws. These representatives can vote according to their judgment and explain to their electorate, if they voted in a way that the electorate would not have supported, why it is that they made that choice. The electorate is not necessarily just electing someone who is not expected to use his or her wisdom or expertise in assessing a piece of legislation, in assessing a proposal, but someone who is expected to use his or her judgment. Otherwise, they could send anybody; if the role was simply to do only what your voters tell you to do and each time there is a piece of legislation, poll your voters and do what they told you, that would be a fairly low-level representation, not requiring judgment, nor expertise.

Of course, people should be informed about your judgment and expertise before they elect you to represent them. Those who are running to become a representative should come up with a program so that the electorate might anticipate how the representative would use his or her judgment and expertise. The electorate should have at least a general idea about where the potential representative would stand on various important issues. Then, of course, the elected representative would be expected to follow up those expectations and vote on various pieces of legislation in a consistent manner, consistent, that is, with the program on the basis of which he or she had been elected.

That's true. It is a relationship between the representative and the constituency. In the past, before modern technologies, the person could explain his or her perspective and the voters would trust that this is the kind of person they want to represent them. That person would go and spend most of the time in the capital and occasionally send information back to the voters or they would read in the newspapers about what has happened in the capital. There was not necessarily a regular ongoing communication between the person who has been sent there and the electorate.

There might be a regular newsletter; congressional Representatives and Senators in the United States are able to send official correspondence using only their signature instead of paying for postage to make it easier for them to communicate with their electorate. This communication is expected. We are now beyond the age of letters and stamps. The voters can send e-mails; the representative maintains a web site, which will need to be regularly updated, and there are many other ways in which the person who is elected can communicate with the electorate and vice versa.

If the representative is drafting or supporting legislation that differs from positions he had taken when he was running for office (it's not that the person's hands are tied and he or she cannot do something different than what he pledged to do), he or she would be expected to talk with the electorate and explain the reason for changing his or her mind. The role is not simply to think for themselves and do what they think is right and never talk with the electorate. They have to be able to explain what they are doing and why they are doing it.

One of the epithets of President Reagan was "the Great Communicator." Whatever people thought with regard to his policies, with regard to his expertise as a decision-maker—he was known to delegate—he was able to communicate why he was doing what he was doing. This helped him significantly to build that rapport, to build that relationship with his supporters and with those with whom he disagreed about the vision that he followed. This requires good communication skills and a sense of trust that you are open. People need to feel that they understand what you're saying, that you'll be truthful with them, and if they have questions, they can ask them and they will get an answer. That is even more the case now that we have moved into this century where we have even more tools to accomplish what I just described. People expect to be in communication, and while sometimes they may expect that those whom they have elected will rigidly follow what the electorate tells them to do, it also depends upon their trust in the wisdom and leadership of the person they have elected. If there is a person whom they don't trust, they will watch that person to see that he or she does exactly as he or she is told to do.

Why would they elect someone whom they don't trust in the first place?

If, after the election, the person builds up a reputation for not doing what the electorate had expected him or her to do and not explain it, then they may try to hold that person to account. This also gets to the greater empowerment that citizens now have with modern tools—to be able to know what their leaders are doing. That leads to a discussion about the changing relationship between the electorate and the elected. A system where everything is decided by plebiscite may be too unwieldy. Instead, it is better to have people whose wisdom you trust and who are open with you and communicate with you, and let them discuss things internally, negotiate, come to some agreement, which the public will accept in the greater interest of all citizens. The ability to communicate all the details at all stages of such negotiations, the ability to see raw data, can also lead to greater polarization. There may be a stronger division of opinions, and people may not want to trust those whom they have elected, and they'd rather tell them how to act. This requires greater sophistication regarding how to work with information.

Why is there reluctance sometimes to be transparent? Why do people who are conducting scientific experiments say, "We don't want to release the results too early." Or they may say, "We'd rather wait till we have more time to assess the results." Whereas someone who is advocating transparency might say, "No, everything that you're doing, every experiment, every success, every failure, every piece of data should be out there from the very beginnings so that the public at large can see what's going on within these labs." The counter argument may be that people may not understand and they may come to the wrong conclusion. It may be too early, and it won't be possible to arrive at a result that would be beneficial to everyone, so let's wait. Finding a balance between being comfortable with opening up your information even at the early stages, and for the public to understand that this is open information and the things have not yet been determined, and that while they have the right now to express their concern and their opinion, this is still a discussion. It is not the case that one side has already made a decision and the public is disenfranchised, nor is it one where the public, seeing raw data, should become overly exercised and make demands based upon that raw data.

Would you be able to estimate the fraction of the population that is interested in this?

I don't have an estimate of how many people are interested in information per se. People generally focus on local issues. As we look at the United States, we are talking about a very large territory, fifty states and each state divided into counties, municipalities, and districts. Most people have local concerns. They want to see what their town council is doing; to understand the factors behind how the police are being deployed in their city; what are the difficulties for garbage collection; why are the taxes being raised; what are the different proposals that affect them directly within their localities and within their state. The farther away something is, the less interest there is. When things happen in Washington, DC that affect people directly in their cities, there is greater interest. If it is with regards to employment, with regards to education, with regards to wages, things that affect people's daily lives, there is greater interest. The economy is something that people are usually concerned about. Why are we paying taxes? Where is this money going? Do we want our government to use our tax money in this way? With regards to foreign policy, our engagement in other countries, whether it is assistance to develop other countries or military engagement, the interest is not quite the same as in local matters. There is interest depending upon what the person's focus is. Some are more interested in international affairs than others, but the percentage is lower.

You have gained a great deal of experience on a broad international scale. In your judgment, do people understand the United States and its policies the way you intend them to understand?

In many ways, they do understand that the United States wants to represent freedom and democracy. The United States still has a very strong image and reputation as a country that symbolizes liberty and human rights. People in many countries feel that they have this close connection with the United States. Many have families, many have relatives who live in the US, and many have travelled to the US and come back. It's hard to be in a country where you don't run into people who have family in the United States. They have this direct connection and hear about what's happening in the United States. They focus also on what the United States is doing, because it is a great super-power in the world and people want the United States to be interested in their concerns. In going to different countries, I find that many people in those countries focus on the United States. They'll have questions about US policies, and they'll be very focused on the United States, much more than Americans might be focused on their country. Some feel dismayed because they feel that the US is not paying as much attention to their country as they are paying to the US. Or, they may disagree with America's policies and ask "when you are presenting yourself as human rights and freedom, force for peace and prosperity, and stability, why are you doing this and this, and this?"

This happened throughout the 20th century until now, whatever the top-ics of the day are. It could have been the civil rights movement in the 1960s; it could have been the perceived abuse of government power in the 1970s, which led to Nixon's resignation; the role we played in the Vietnam War; the bat-tle against communism. People see these things in different ways. The fight against terrorism and the use of surveillance in order to provide better intelli-gence for security; where are the lines and where are the limits? These are ques-tions people outside the United States ask about the United States in the same way that people in the United States ask questions about these issues. Many people outside the United States get their understanding of what is happening in the United States by looking at what Americans are saying about themselves. By virtue of the fact that we have relative openness in our government, they can get information from the US government about what the US government is doing as well as from civil society and other watchdogs that analyze governance in the US. and disseminate their comments. These discussions that would normally be domestic discussions about US policy, become very international discussions.

As diplomats, in representing our country, we are primarily trying to explain US policy. In our public comments, we are generally not focusing on what is happening internally in the country where we happen to be. However, by saying that transparency, accountability, human rights, and engagements with citizens are good goals, that these are goals that we in the United States strive for, that we want to achieve, we are also making the case that all good governments would want to achieve these same goals. If we don't meet our own expectations, they can criticize us, and they can criticize us if we expect others to meet these goals that we ourselves are not meeting. That becomes part of our discussion when we talk about shared goals; where we are saying, yes, we agree that we should all work together towards these goals. If our partners are trying to avoid achieving these goals, they could say, "Look at you, let's talk about you first, let's see whether the United State is achieving those goals that you're saying are our common goals." However, the goal is not to point fingers at each other's shortcomings, but to work toward the type of society we envision for ourselves. In doing so, we also need to recognize that we ourselves have areas in which we need to improve, and the first step toward improving is in acknowledging our weaknesses rather than trying to hide them. We recognize our faults and recognize that we, in the United States, should do better, we must do better, and we can all do better. Let's do better, together. Some countries would rather not have these discussions about doing better together, but may want to continue to focus on the faults in others. Such an approach hinders mutual progress.

Speaking about the United States, we have to recognize that we are fifty states. Many outside the United States, those who focus on the US and want the US to pay attention to them, say that Americans don't understand the rest of the world because we don't know about all the different countries. However, viewing the United States as similar to other countries, and similar to one of their neighbors, may not be recognizing the complexity of the United States and its system. It is a union of states, a country based on a union of fifty states, each of which has its own government, and each of which has a sense of some autonomy. Each of these states has ceded part of its sovereignty to the federal government in Washington; and we have worked for two hundred years to come to this unified national identity. We work together as harmoniously as possible and we have succeeded so well in presenting ourselves as a unified country that many outside the United States will see us as a single entity in the same way as other countries are single entities. In reality, we have to coordinate fifty different states. Some call themselves commonwealths, others call themselves states; some have unicameral legislatures, others have bicameral legislatures. They all have governors, which are equivalent to a head of state. Occasionally there is even talk in some states of leaving the union. We fought a civil war to keep our union together. It is a very complex system, which can be compared in simplistic ways to other single states, but in other ways, it should be compared to unions of states. It is also a model of how to work together; how states with different perspectives—some are conservative, some are agricultural, some are progressive, and some are very urban—can find unity in shared values. Our states have different types of educational systems; they have different ethnic mixes, and different historical backgrounds; yet, despite the differences, we can find a great deal of commonality and a great sense of purpose of what it means to be Americans, what we believe in, and we work together in a way that shows unity to the rest of the world.

Hungarian Experience

When you arrived in Hungary, was there an ambassador?

No. The ambassador had left in July 2013; I arrived in August.

When you left Hungary, was there an ambassador?

The ambassador arrived in January 2015; I left in February.

You went to Hungary as Deputy Chief of Mission (DCM).

When I asked for the assignment, I assumed, I would be going in a deputy position under an ambassador.

Was DCM your title throughout?

That was my official title. However, there is always somebody who is the chief of the mission in charge of the embassy. If the ambassador is not there, the deputy becomes the person in charge. If the ambassador and the deputy are not there, then the next highest-ranking person becomes the person in charge of the embassy. We all have a career rank, similar to the military. We have different sections in the embassy; there is a political section, a public affairs section, an economic section, a management section, a consular section, and each of those positions is filled by a person who has a rank.

The title of the person in charge of the embassy, when there is no ambassador, is Chargé d'Affaires. Usually this title is followed by "ad interim." The Chargé d'Affaires is not an official title; it is a designation to indicate who is in charge at any given time, because there always has to be somebody in charge of the embassy.

When I was in Syria, there was no ambassador, so the deputy chief of mission there was also the Chargé d'Affaires. That was for a much longer period; we did not have an ambassador for about five years. I was the head of the consular section there and I was also the next highest in rank. When the Chargé was away, that is, when the deputy chief of mission was away, I became the Chargé in Damascus. In Budapest, the person after me who had the highest rank was the head of the political section. When I was away, that person became the Chargé d'Affaires.

When you arrived, did you anticipate being the Chargé d'Affaires of the US embassy in Budapest?

For a short time. When I arrived, the ambassador had not yet been nominated and I knew that the previous ambassador would be leaving in July; at some point, it was still a question, how long she would stay. When I arrived in August, I knew she would not be there. Her deputy was there when I arrived, and we overlapped for about a week. Then he left, and I became the Chargé d'Affaires.

What is a normal period for not having an ambassador?

There is no normal period; there was a relatively long gap between Ambassador April Foley and Ambassador Eleni Tsakopoulos Kounalakis, from April 2, 2009 to January 7, 2010; it was about a year.

I don't think many people noticed that gap; but many noticed the period between 2013 and 2015. A prolonged absence of ambassador is a statement.

I just wanted to say that in Syria, the five-year gap was more of a statement. The Senate was not willing to send an ambassador to Syria at that time. In Hungary and most other countries where we did not have an ambassador, it was not a statement. The reason was the bureaucratic process of nominating an ambassador, having the person go through the hearing, and having a full Senate vote on the appointment. What happened for many embassies at the end of 2013 and in 2014, was a different kind of statement. There were differences between the parties in Congress. The minority party at the time, the Republican Party, made a statement with regards to the speed by which the executive appointments were processed. The executive appointments are senior-level appointments, and they have to go through the Senate. Many appointments were delayed, were held up during that time.

The hold-up began in December 2013 and continued through the elections, which took place in November 2014. They had occasional hearings, but moved very slowly. By summer 2014, some sixty or even more ambassadorial appointments were vacant. There were articles in the major newspapers in the United States about this. We barely managed to send an ambassador to Russia before the end of summer 2014, before the Senate went on recess. Finally, the Senate recognized the importance of having an ambassador in Moscow at this critical time. The situation was so difficult that the Secretary of State took the unusual step of writing an editorial about this situation, which was making it difficult for the United States to be represented at the level at which it needs to be represented. Then, after the elections, they began to move more quickly on approving ambassadors. The ambassador to Hungary was confirmed in December 2014 and arrived in January. Thus, the delay in this case was not a statement with respect to Hungary and it was not something that I expected. I just had to do my best in representing the United States during this period.

It was an unusual period.

When is it a usual period?

What I mean is that you took an activist role; this was unusual.

What do you mean by *activist*? I have something in mind, but tell me what you mean by that.

You initiated things, did not wait for detailed instructions for what to do, and gained visibility.

This somewhat reflects the changing nature of communication, a variety of factors, and personality, too. Conversations are important and I keep returning to this theme. This has been a driving premise with regards to how I engaged with people throughout my career. This is how I functioned in Tel Aviv, New Delhi, and Moscow. Then, I was much more junior with regard to my rank, and therefore, much less visible, but the technologies were also different. Conversation does create a rapport. If a person goes out and has a conversation, like you and I are having now, it establishes a different kind of rapport than only going out when it is necessary to make a speech, only going out in a very official capacity and not being able to appear approachable, not showing genuine interest in what's happening around you. It is important to be able to relax, to be able to converse, and not just have a conversation, but find the right way to have it. A conversation can be very informal, very casual, in fact, so informal that people of other cultures may not understand what you're talking about, or may not understand the nuances or the Americanisms. The casualness of the conversation may also be taken as a sign of disrespect if it is too casual. Or, the person can be so excessively formal that it does not look like you're talking to a real person; rather, as if the person would be reading from a piece of paper. Finding some place in the middle where you're able to say what you intend to say in a way that is culturally understandable, regardless where you are, takes some time and some effort. You need to build up that rapport before you actually start to communicate.

One of my interests in my academic studies was communication and communication theory as well. There are different models of communication, whether it's a two-step flow of communication, or the uses and gratification theory of communication; there are many different models for communication. Some of the early models posited that the only thing that prevented a strong communicator from persuading people to do what he or she wanted was the amount of interference that conflicted with the message. This was along the lines of radio communications. There is a signal. What's the interference; and then in the end, what elements of that message can still be understood? What's missing in those early models is the feedback. In the old days, you might remember we used to use a modem to connect to the Internet; you had to attach it to the telephone, and there was a noise before you were actually connected. That noise was analogous to "a handshake" as one's computer and the Internet system determined whether they could communicate with each other effectively. This was technological communication drawing from the human rapport-building aspect of a handshake. The same thing applies to conversation. When people greet each other, the first few words don't mean anything except that they establish a rapport. "Hello, how are you?" If you understood what I said, you respond back with a culturally appropriate response. If you stare at me blankly, then I know that you didn't understand what I said, or that you interpreted it in a way that does not let you give the response that I'm expecting. We continue until it looks like, in fact, we have established some communication where, if I say something, you respond back in a way that I expect, and then you say something, and I understand what you are saying. It's only after that, that real communication can take place. Only after you establish a common understanding, a rapport, with your audience that you can have a conversation.

You are saying that wherever you went, you exercised the same approach, let it be Tel Aviv, New Delhi, Moscow, Damascus, or Budapest.

Yes, in talking to people.

Did your experience in Hungary stand out in any way among your interactions with people in these five stations?

The response was similar. Some people are friendlier than others, but it was my role that was different. The types of conversations I had and the authoritativeness with which I could speak were different within each country. In Tel Aviv, New Delhi, Moscow, then a number of African countries, in Britain, or in Syria, there were similarities and there were differences. Going out, going to the marketplace, walking down the street, going to a restaurant, meeting with friends, meeting with contacts, and just talking. There were many commonalities with regard to how we interact as humans. There were many different ways that we understood and felt things in common or that we could come to an understanding if we just rephrased things a little bit differently. It is also a learning process to pick up the nuances, learning to understand what the person was saying back to me. This way, we were able to shape the conversation in a way that we both understood what we were saying, and the direction in which we were going. This was important in all those places.

In Hungary, at the outset, I continued to have conversations and I was fairly low profile. Most people don't know the deputy chiefs of mission of an embassy; even many of the ambassadors are not really well known. I arrived in August 2013 and for six months, in October, November, December, I could go to places and people walked by me and did not recognize me. I would talk with people; I would engage them in conversation trying to understand what was happening in Hungarian society, and how Hungarians understood what was happening in Hungarian society. I was happy to talk about the perspective of the United States and the US embassy and what was happening in the United States. I wanted to open up the doors of the embassy even more and have conversations with the public using other technologies, not just only talking to groups of ten or twenty people or having a conversation with ten or twenty people, or giving a talk to a larger audience of a hundred people or two hundred people. I wanted to have conversations with larger numbers of people, and I asked the embassy if there was a way we could do this using social media.

In December 2013, we set up a "Talk to the Chargé" web-chat on the Internet. This was not something that we were doing in Hungary before. When I was in Damascus, we set up at "Talk to the Consul" web-chat on the Internet. We did the same thing in Britain as well, using this technology to talk to the Consul, trying to find ways to engage the public. You'll find numerous other US embassies doing something similar on the Internet. Using the Internet to have a conversation for an hour or so is not uncommon; more and more of our diplomats are doing that.

It took a lot of work, it was fairly labor-intensive: working with a very dedicated public affairs team, to sit there and try to manage the incoming inquiries and write a response back quickly. I wanted something that would be more casual, and more of an ongoing conversation. So, in January 2014, I started a blog. The purpose was not so much to comment on what was going on in Hungary—it is not our role. I was trying to find an appropriate title for my blog to express our intention to get across and engage in conversation with regard to people understanding each other's culture and bridging the existing gaps. This is why I called my blog "Civil Voices." This was, in one way, a reflection of the importance of civil society, but also, being civil. Speaking civilly means that you understand that there were going to be differences of opinion, but it's important in a diverse society to exercise civility and not throw stones at each other when you speak. I was using my blog to talk about American society, American culture.

My first blog entry was on Martin Luther King Day and I reflected on civil rights in the United States, on the diversity of society in the United States, on the different influences that have come together in building the type of society we have in the US. The next post to my blog was on music, on how we sometimes use folk music to shape our society. It was the anniversary of the death of Stephen Foster (1826–1864) who wrote many songs that people around the world recognize and think of as archetypal American songs, like "My Old Kentucky Home" or "Oh! Susanna." These songs were written by someone who had only visited the South once. He lived in New York, yet was known for creating this very nostalgic, romantic view of life in the southern United States before the Civil War. He was shaping this vision in his music of this ante-bellum or pre-Civil War South. How accurate was his vision? Was it simply a myth that we create about ourselves through our folk culture—I was talking about this in my second blog post. Whatever I was saying about the culture of the United States, people could relate it to their own culture as well.

I did not just want to use the blog, however, as a platform to hear my own voice talking about things in an informal and casual way, but I wanted to use it to engender discussion. However, not many people were writing on it, and not many were commenting. I was not getting as much response as I'd hoped for, and it did take time for me to write that blog. I was doing it twice a month and it went on in January, February, March, and on. In July, I thought that perhaps I should use Twitter. By then, more and more people were using Twitter to communicate, and I had never used it before. It was an experiment for me, but it was a way to have a conversation. I picked July 4 as a good day to start—America's National Day—and started by simply referencing various things that I was doing. Our official party, the formal large gathering was on the 3rd and it was a work day, but the 4th was a holiday, a day to spend with our families and to celebrate our independence. We had an embassy gathering and it was the last time we were using the Marine House in Buda for this celebration. So, my first tweet was about celebrating the Fourth of July Holiday with my colleagues. My tweet was nothing provocative; it was nothing conspicuous, just a good starting tweet.

In my tweets, I thought it was appropriate to be open and transparent about what we do as diplomats. What is our role here? Are we just attending fancy parties or are we doing other things that are worth mentioning. This was how I initially began using Twitter to highlight the things I was doing as Chargé d'Affaires in Budapest. It was also a means for conversation, because people could write back; they could comment on what I was tweeting. As I began to use it more, I didn't want to just give statements about what I was doing, but also, to reflect informally on what I was seeing. Would people be interested in that? Again, I tried not to comment too much or directly on things that were happening in Hungary, but to provide a perspective on how I viewed various events taking place. The conversations could be interesting. Sometimes there was criticism of the United States in response to my comments and sometimes there was a lot of support.

In September, civil society was being audited within Hungary and there were other concerns with regards to the state of civil society. This was when President Obama made a speech on September 23, 2014, in which he mentioned Hungary as one of the countries in which civil society was under threat, and we have already talked about it. So, I had comments about the importance of civil society within any country, within a democracy. My comment was not necessarily about Hungary, but these statements are held to be self-evident. In a democracy, it is important to value civil society. I would sometimes provide links in my tweets to documents highlighting how we were reproached at various times. Sometimes these tweets were humorous, again, highlighting what was going on in my daily life.

After the United States found six Hungarians ineligible to enter the United States, under Presidential Proclamation 7750, for engaging in corrupt activity, I tried not to be brought into a discussion about Hungarian domestic politics. There was a discussion about having the US provide more information about the banned individuals, but instead we tried to keep the discussion focused on accountability or what are we doing in the United States. One of my tweets linked to a report that the Department of Justice provides every year to the Congress—on American officials that had been found guilty of corrupt activity. Again, I highlighted openness with regard to this information about how we approach corruption and accountability within the United States. The report is available on-line and everybody can see it. Having this level of transparency builds confidence among American citizens that their officials are held accountable; and this document was something that I could link to on the Internet. This showed that we take corruption in the United States as seriously, if not more seriously, than elsewhere.

After that, and many people saw this on a video posted to the Internet, I met with the head of the tax authority of Hungary. My tweet about this was that I'd had an unexpected visit by the tax authority. Many people commented on this encounter using humor, treating it as a humorous event, which, I suppose, in some ways, if one can detach oneself from the gravity of the issues themselves, it was.

Was this meeting a turning point in your enhanced visibility?

Around that time, in September- October, people were seeing me in more places. My face was on television more; I was in the newspapers more. I had been spending a lot of time explaining why it is that we value civil society, why it is that we think accountability is important, why we think corruption is a threat to democratic society, to the stability of society. I'd become very recognizable by October. Of course, that particular video –

Who made that video?

It was the TV crew that was there.

How did they happen to be there?

You can ask them. It was Hír TV. What happened was that I was going out of the embassy for a walk. I'd just finished a meeting and the weather was nice; it was good to step outside. I came out and as I was passing the front of the embassy, I saw two people standing there. They looked vaguely familiar, but I was not going to pause and ask, do I know you? I just kept walking and I walked past the Soviet monument, the monument to the fallen soldiers that is there. As I was doing that, a cameraman came up to me with a reporter. It looked as if the reporter wanted to interview me, but this is not how one schedules an interview with anyone, let alone with the head of an embassy. We have a press office, if they had wanted an interview, and I'd given plenty of interviews, they could have scheduled one with our press office. So, I continued walking and told them that I am sorry but I am not going to give an interview right now. I would have thought that was enough if that was all they were looking for, but they continued to follow me, and I wasn't sure why they were following me. Then the reporter asked, "why are you leaving the embassy when the head of the tax authority is here to see you?" That was the first that I realized that she had come there to see me, and I stopped. This is all on tape and you can guess what's going on in my mind. We were standing there in the middle of the square and we had a conversation there and it was being filmed by the crew of Hír TV. It was for broadcast; the raw footage was also apparently made available, and people could watch it on Hír TV and elsewhere as well. It was news footage that was published.

Did you ever feel gratitude to the head of the tax authority?

Gratitude? Why would I feel gratitude?

Didn't she do a great service for you? Didn't she help you in gaining more access to the public, even if this was not her goal?

In some ways, it was good to see that I was able to engage in a conversation with the public and that more people were interested in having these conversations with me and the embassy. They felt that we were actually explaining the basis of what we were doing fairly well, and we had gained access to the media, from the conservative media to the progressive media, which was unusual. *Magyar Nemzet* did a very large interview with me, even earlier, a full page. They didn't tone it down, there was a pretty good exchange between me and the reporter. *Heti Válasz* as well as *Népszabadság* did an interview with me, *Blikk*, and other papers. I was in many different print media, as well as on-line media. Interest did continue to grow; people were laughing with me, or at me in some cases. Having a meaningful conversation means that you can't always take yourself seriously. In conversations with you and in conversations with anyone else, you have got to be prepared to sit together and laugh with each other, which helps create the rapport that you need for a good conversation. This is like having a drink with each other.

You became more famous at least in part due to that encounter on Szabadság Square. The head of the tax authority went to see you without an appointment and when she met you, she asked for an interpreter; this became such a popular story that made you into a household figure.

People had tried to read a lot into her coming, why was a TV camera there, et cetera. People can speculate. I never asked her, why?

You said she came accompanied by someone.

Her attorney. We went into the embassy and spoke for a couple of hours. She gave an interview afterwards to the media, but I'd rather not talk about that private meeting.

Of course, people can't just walk into the embassy and talk with the head of the embassy or anybody else for that matter; it is not even possible to walk into that building.

If I have time to talk with somebody, I am happy to talk.

On the square, how did you communicate?

In English. The reporter or the cameraman translated for her. After she left the embassy, the TV crew was still there. Someone asked her, how it was that a TV crew was there, and she didn't know. She said, they were just there.

Was there any consequence of the meeting?

After that meeting, it was harder for me to have quiet conversations and to go places and not be recognized. I liked to go places and see what the mood of the country was, what the mood of the city was. Now I was a recognized figure.

When I asked you if you felt gratitude to her, of course, it was not a serious question, but she did help you become known.

She, or, rather, that incident, and the whole incident with regards to the United States making a statement—that accountability is important. And, if we do identify corrupt government officials, we can take particular actions according to US law, such as not letting those people into the United States—that's what the United States can do. And, as I pointed out in our previous conversation, our Open Government National Action Plan is one of the documents in which we advocate using visa ineligibility in countering corruption. In this case, we did it. This action prompted a discussion in Hungarian society about the nature of corruption and about the nature of accountability. That was a good discussion to take place; helping people to expect accountability, to expect that their officials will be held to the same laws that they are.

Did the encounter amplify your message?

The episode may have amplified another aspect as well, of people beginning to find humor in daily life.

That sounds like an exaggeration—to ascribe this much to that meeting.

The discussion about corruption and accountability was taking place beforehand. It continued afterwards, so there it did not mean much change. What changed was some of the tone. There were numerous Internet memes, as they are called, after that, most of them humorous, some with me as a caricature, some with her as a caricature. Slogans appeared. People were finding ways to inject humor into this very difficult situation in which they were seeing that maybe there is not accountability and that there should be. They saw that the relationship between citizens and government is not what it should be. They saw that they are not empowered in the way they would expect as citizens, but they could empower themselves through humor.

Can you positively state that you did not stage the episode yourself?

I did not stage it. [Laughing] What the story showed was that circumstances can change at any time. You have to be able to assess the situation and not just react; you engage with it, be part of it, and try to shape it, together with your partners. Getting back to conversation, people valued this window into my life. I am now talking about Twitter and that I was communicating regularly and would answer people when they would write. Sometimes there were people who I'd never met; others may have been well-known people within FIDESZ. For example, George Schöpflin and I regularly engaged in conversation on Twitter and it was a good-natured clashing of wits, and it was very public.

When the demonstration concerning the Internet tax was taking place, and I'd heard that it was going to be fairly large, I had something else scheduled earlier on that day, the commemoration of Cardinal Mindszenty in Felsőpetény, the town where he'd been held captive under the communists. He was released and [eventually] came to the American embassy for shelter. I went to this commemoration earlier; and it was an interesting gathering, fairly conservative, where people did not speak English. I tried to engage with them in Hungarian. I was able to have some conversation in Hungarian about why we were saying what we were saying. I was happy to find people who were critical of our policy and critical of me. They were silent initially, as we were walking along from the church to the castle, the building where he was held. As we were walking, I said a few words in Hungarian and they said a few words back. It was clear that they did not like what we were doing. "Why are you telling Hungary what to do?" they asked me. "You've elected President Obama; we've elected Prime Minister Orbán. We make our own decisions, why are you telling us what we should do?" That was a good starting point for a conversation, because in my mind, we weren't telling Hungary what to do. This was again with regards to the accountability issue, the corruption issue. I told them that we did what we needed to do and that Hungary should do what its citizens wanted it to do. The government should respond to its own citizens and not respond to the United States. I agreed with them, "You've elected this government, this government needs to be responsive to you; we won't tell this government what to do; you need to tell your government what to do, what the right thing is," This was a way, again, to have a conversation with those who might misconstrue our message. I spent several hours there talking and stayed to the end of the commemoration. Then, we went back to the town for the reception they had there, and talked with more people about their perspectives.

Then, I came back to Budapest and it was soon time to take a look at this demonstration about the Internet tax. I went thinking that I could be relatively inconspicuous, staying around the periphery of the gathering to see how many people there were, what kind of things they were saying, what the mood in this environment was. From where I was, I was seeing parents with children, older people, younger people, a very big mix of people. Then, I moved along Andrássy út to Heroes' Square and I went to see how everything progressed. I left before it was finished. When I saw how much they filled up Heroes'

Square, it gave me an idea of the size, and then I left. As I was leaving, when I was already in the car, I received a Twitter message from a reporter, "Were you at that demonstration?" I said, I went and watched it, yes. The reporter responded that there were pictures of me there. I said when I get back to my house I'll post my own pictures, which I did.

I got back, I tweeted that earlier that day I went to the Mindszenty commemoration and later to the Internet tax demonstration. That launched a conversation with the government spokesperson, Zoltán Kovács. He was critical of my having gone there. It was even more telling that each of our tones in the conversation was very different, and people picked up on that. I write on Twitter in a way that is similar to the way I'm talking with you. I'm trying to not be too casual, nor too formal, but somewhere in the middle, recognizing that this is public discussion. Discussing why I went there, I tried to explain that it's important to see what's happening in Hungary, that diplomats have a responsibility to understand the mood in the country. This discussion was in public; there were reporters at the time who began also commenting on this discussion reminding Kovács that what he's saying is very public. Does he realize it? There was nothing necessarily wrong with what he was saying, because it was a difference in opinion. What people were commenting on was the tone: the very pointed tone he was taking whereas I was trying to have a conversation. This particular exchange was then reported in *The New York Times*, in other international media, as well as widely reported in the Hungarian press. This exchange was on Twitter between the head of the American embassy and the spokesperson of the government of Hungary. Again, this is a new environment in which we're all learning the dynamics of how to have this kind of conversation. It also highlighted for me that I could no longer expect to be anonymous or incognito, regardless where I go. If I go to any kind of gathering, I am going to be recognized. I still tried to get out and meet with people, but always now with the understanding that I was very much a recognized figure in Hungary.

Another anecdote illuminates this point about how the media have changed things. On New Year's Eve, or not quite, maybe on December the 30th, at the Széchenyi Bath they had a New Year's lightshow party; something for young people. The steam from the bath, the laser lights made this very mysterious. My youngest son was visiting with a friend, and they wanted to go there. For me, this was an opportunity as well. I had not been to a party like that, and I thought it would be interesting to go and see what it was like. Thus, I went with my son and his friend to the Széchenyi Bath at eleven o'clock at night. I stayed through midnight, until one o'clock and maybe I came back at two o'clock in the morning. My son and his friend stayed until it finished at three. When I came back, I wanted to read a little bit before going to sleep. *The Economist* magazine online happened to have an article about Hungary, about what was happening in the domestic situation, the nature of the government, the concerns with regards to the civil society, the protests; all the things that were happening. The article mentioned me, but in the comments following the article, there were people writing, some of them from England, some were supportive of the government and a couple of them were critical of my role, of me going out to various places and speaking with people, expressing my opinion on Twitter, and so forth. Somebody else wrote in response to that comment in *The Economist* that people seem to like what Goodfriend is doing. He gets around, goes and sees different places; in fact, just tonight he was at the Széchenyi Bath with his children. I thought this was incredible. I've just now come back from the Bath and already somebody who was there and recognized me—and in the steam, it was hard to recognize anybody—and who reads *The Economist* as well, had already posted a comment in *The Economist* about where I was and what I'd done. This showed that the attention was enormous.

Shortly before, on Christmas Day, I posted Christmas greetings, expressing hope for a peaceful year; something like that. Major media in Hungary reported that I was hoping for a peaceful year. The conversations, the rapport that I'd managed to build with different members of society, the genuine sense of openness, the willingness to discuss things, to hear things, to understand what was happening, to be an American there, but one who is truly concerned about our relationship and our common desire to achieve these noble goals, it had resonated throughout many different segments of society. These private conversations—and by private, I don't mean secret—these informal conversations, going out and talking with different people, became part of other media and everything supported everything else. There was a national discussion going on and I was a big part of it without having to say a lot.

In science, we call this a cooperative effect when initially small effects get multiplied very rapidly through interactions. When did you learn that you had to return to the United States?

It was not related to the situation in Hungary at all; it was a personal decision I had to make.

Had it been an operational decision, it would have also been logical to avoid upstaging the functioning of the new Ambassador.

But it was really a family circumstance.

Then it was a fortunate coincidence.

From my perspective, the fact that we had an ambassador in place made it easier for me to make the choice to address the family matter that we had.

Would you like to visit Hungary again?

I would; very much so.

A Current Issue

Before we started our conversations, we agreed that our focus would not be on current political events. However, as we are recording our conversations in the middle of September 2015, it is impossible not to ask about your thoughts concerning the migration and refugee situation that we are observing in Europe, including Hungary. There is profound complexity in this unprecedented flood of people coming from the Middle East and Afghanistan. This is something new, but sometimes, looking at the people, many of them with small children, and in some of the scenes, there is also a déjà vu feeling, as if I had already seen this. I am quoting from a description of a scene in June 1944—after we had boarded the cattle carriages of the train whose original destination was Auschwitz. My brother described the scene in the 1990s; at the time of the journey, he was ten years old; I was not yet three. "The carriages were so crowded that we all had to be standing. A pail was placed in one of the corners and the carriage was locked. The gendarme then appeared and distributed very spicy sausage and onions. There was no bread and no water. They called us dogs and fed us like dogs, and we all ate the sausage and the gendarmes were laughing. The train stood and people were losing their minds from being thirsty and they could not make it to the pail and within a few hours there was already the first dead in our carriage."[12] This scene came to my mind when I saw the video with the Hungarian police throwing bread packages to the migrants/refugees. In the carriage, at least there was no fighting for the food; whereas in the video, there was. I could not see the faces of the police and I don't know if they were enjoying themselves.

---

12 Istvan Hargittai, *Our Lives: Encounters of a Scientist* (Budapest: Akadémiai Kiadó, 2004), 52.

The current migration has been described as the largest since World War II. With regards to transparency, openness, and some of the differences between these periods, if you think, what we knew in real time of what was actually happening in the 1940s, if we just take the movement of the displaced people after World War II; people moving to different places, it was hard to have real time information. Everything happened in isolated places. It was only afterwards that we could identify what the movements were. The United States saw the Europeans in such disarray at the time; this was the genesis of the Marshall Plan. It tried to assist so that Europe would not crumble under the weight of these conditions. Clearly, some assistance was needed to help Europe rebuild and to cope with the huge changes that had been taking place. But we weren't able to act in a unified way with regard to all of the people's movements that were taking place and the suffering that was happening at the very micro level. Things could be happening in secret that we didn't know about. The suffering that was taking place, deprivation that was taking place; that did not come out until later. We might hit ourselves now, why couldn't we address these things? Why didn't we know about these things? We didn't have the same tools for communication, for transparency, for openness then, as we do now. If you look at what's happening now, just from the perspective of transparency, we can see in almost real time what is happening in all of these places; and we are trying to connect the various dots while the situation is actually happening. Some points are directing us to see what's happening in North Africa, in the Middle East. We can see the issues that are causing the people's movements there. Let's address that part, because we can see what's happening there. These issues are in the news regularly; different groups are posting videos of what they're doing. We understand the suffering and the disarray in those countries and the issues facing people in the refugee camps in Turkey, in Jordan, or in Lebanon. There is a desire to provide some assistance there. We know the paths people are taking throughout the Middle East and going to Greece or coming up to the Balkans into Central Europe. We face the question: how can we address these issues? There are news items on twenty-four-hour a day news channels and on the Internet as well. Then, we see the migrants arriving, again, in real time. We see the pictures that you spoke about, of how they are treated as they arrive in Hungary or as they arrive in Austria or in Germany, and how the treatment differs from place to place. The migrants themselves post videos; there are many working as volunteers trying to assist these migrants and they post videos too; NGOs go and inspect the conditions, write their assessments in real time and immediately publish those assessments, and governments react via public statements. All of this is happening in real time, in a very public, open way. We are being asked, how can we address this? How can we deal with these issues now as they are happening, in order to prevent mistreatment, in order to hold people accountable, in order to make preparations for the appropriate treatment of people who have suffered so much? This change, when you have volunteers organizing themselves effectively, counting the numbers, knowing what is needed in different places, knowing which roads are closed, is the empowerment of citizens.

Civil society appears to be better equipped—which it is not, in reality— than the machinery of the government in dealing with this crisis.

What you're saying is that you as an observer, because of your ability to see what is happening, are noticing the disparity, and seeing that the volunteers are filling a role that we might have expected governments to fill. You are seeing governments, that had time to prepare, act in ways that you would not expect and you don't support. You feel that you are in a position to understand what is happening and to express an informed opinion. This is what transparency can assist with. It facilitates citizen participation and engagement. You can express an informed opinion, because you have the information at the same time as the government has.

What you're saying even makes the contrast sharper.

It enables citizens to hold their government accountable. This is what I have been saying before. Transparency and engagement of civil society enables citizens to play the active role in their society that they need to play. This puts responsibility on the citizens as well. If they choose to ignore the information they have access to and let government do what it wants without shouldering their responsibility as engaged citizens, that's a reflection on society as well. Civil society may recognize the need for emergency measures under the circumstances of the situation and may understand the need for security. However, it also may expect the government to be adequately prepared to work with desperate people in a humane way and expect civility and a humanitarian approach from its government. That being said, open government also enables people to work more effectively in partnership with government. Ideally, NGOs, commercial enterprises, government and the general public should work together as partners in a climate where they share information with each other.

There is so much information that citizens have now to both facilitate effective public-private partnerships and to hold governments accountable. In this era of openness and transparency, governments need to be able to address this information and promote transparency to say, "this is not how we expect our officials to act," and rather than hide their actions from you, we are going to promote even greater transparency. This will help all government officials act in a way that is condoned by the government and condoned by the citizens.

Personal History

Keeping with your tacit desire to hold yourself in the background, we have not talked much about you, your family, and your life. As we are nearing the end of our conversation, I'm sure there is a great deal of interest— I know, I am curious myself—to learn more about you, about how you became what you became?

I was born in Los Angeles, California, on September 24, 1957. I was a first generation American on my father's side. My father and his parents came to the US in 1949 as refugees from France after WWII. As a Jewish family in France, they were hiding during the war. My paternal grandfather emigrated to France from Poland in the early 1930s. He was a tailor from Złoczew in southern Poland. He had two brothers; one went to Britain and the other to someplace else. I don't know what happened with them. I never met my grandfather's brothers, and he didn't speak much about them. Actually, he didn't speak much about his life before he came to the US at all. I found out much of what I know later through talking with his cousin and with my grandmother, and through genealogical research. My paternal grandfather died in 1980.

My paternal grandmother was from Bialystok, Poland, and she moved to Paris about 1934. She came from a religious family and left Poland to be in a liberal, more open environment. They met in Paris, shortly after she'd arrived, at a large demonstration. Mounted police were chasing away the crowd; she was frightened and asked a man nearby if he spoke Yiddish. He did, and that was my future grandfather. My father was born in Paris in 1935.

When the Nazis invaded in 1940, my father was five years old. My grandmother and my father left for southern France and my father was with a

Christian family and they pretended that he was Christian. My grandfather was with the Polish armed forces, together with my grandmother's brother, and they ended up incarcerated in a prisoner of war camp for a while. After the war, the family reunited and went back to Paris, but they lost their apartment and everything was in disarray, so they came to the US as refugees and joined my grandmother's sister in Los Angeles in 1949.

My mother's family came to the US in different times as well. My mother's father, when he was 11 years old went from Cyprus to Zagazig, Egypt, to live with his brother there. When he was 21, he came to the US in 1919 and joined two others of his brothers who had immigrated at the end of the nineteenth century. They, three brothers, lived in Phoenix, Arizona. My grandfather's oldest brother had a coffee shop, a sweet shop; they made candies from cactus plants. Sometime in the 1920s, my grandfather's oldest brother went to Cyprus to find a wife for my grandfather and brought back my grandmother. Thus, this was an arranged marriage, and they married in Arizona.

My mother was born there in 1929. She studied music, went to the University of Southern California for her Master's degree in music and met my father there at a concert that she was giving. They were married in 1956. My father joined the army and was sent to Alaska, where he went with my mother. After one year, they came back to Los Angeles, where I was born. I have a sister two years younger than me and a brother four years younger than me.

What did your father do?

He did not have a profession prior to joining the army. He occasionally sang and danced on stage. He loves music. He went up to polytechnic, but did not complete college. After the army he worked in air cargo for airlines most of his career. My parents separated when I was four years old, shortly after the birth of my brother. My mother moved back to Phoenix with three children in 1961. My father visited us occasionally until I was eight or nine years old, and then we lost contact with him. I was raised in Phoenix by my mother and her parents.

I had a normal American, urban childhood; I had a newspaper route. I thought I would study sciences; I liked the certainty of science; I was fairly good with math. In high school, I also studied speech and literature. In my first year at the University of Arizona in Tucson, I took some science courses, but I chose to major in philosophy. I wanted to understand human thought; how do we understand the world around us?

Although I'd lost contact with my father, I stayed in contact with his parents who lived in Los Angeles, and through them, I invited my father to my high school graduation, and he came. There was a re-connection. I used to romanticize about why he might have gone, and where he might have gone to, which brought him back into my life in a very poetic way. After he came to my high school graduation, we got to know each other much better.

As I shifted away from science towards philosophy, I added languages to my interests, including classical Greek. I knew that my family came from different places, that things had happened to them in World War II, even in World War I, and that this experience brought with it different cultural perspectives.

Philosophy was my major, I added classical Greek as a second major, and had religious studies as a minor. I had to think about what I was going to do for a profession with classical Greek and philosophy, and I did not want to become just an academic looking at how we understand the world in this intangible way that might be removed from the realities of the world. I asked such questions as, how do we communicate what we are thinking? Thus, I decided to study radio and television, the media, as well. I finished with my college requirements in three years, but decided to stay for two more years. To my previous two majors, I added radio and television as a major and French as a major.

After five years at university, in 1980, I had four bachelor's degrees: three BA degrees and the radio and television degree was a bachelor in fine arts. As a student, I had been working at an all-news radio station for one year. It was interesting to see how news was compiled; we were affiliated with several different networks, and I had the late-night shift. Sometimes, I worked 12 hours at a time, from 7pm until 7am. This experience completely changed my body clock; it's never been the same since. Like many American students and unlike students in many other countries, I worked and studied at the same time. I was working all night; slept for an hour or two before going to classes, and tried to sleep a little in the afternoon. I was very tired much of the time.

When I finished my studies, I was thinking of going into news or documentary film production, but thought, rather than filming about things, how about participating? What's a good way to actually use this education in an applied way, as applied sociology or applied philosophy in governance? How we shape our society around us?

I applied for the Foreign Service. At that time, the State Department was separate from our Information Agency (USIA—United States Information Agency) and since I was interested in the media, I applied for our Information Agency at first. At that time, President Carter had changed the name to US International Communication Agency, shifting the focus from putting out information to communicating, which attracted me. It implied having an actual dialog rather than a one-way flow of information. I applied and there was a series of tests. I passed the tests and was on the list of candidates for the communication agency. At the same time, I went down to Guatemala to study Spanish. When I returned, I was told that I'd made the list for acceptance, except that now our new president, Ronald Reagan, had frozen the funding for Federal agencies to hire new people. I was on the list, waiting to be taken into government service, but they weren't hiring. Also, they had changed the name back to the US Information Agency.

I went on a trip to Europe and traveled on a Eurail Pass with my mother. Then, I came back to the US and my paternal grandfather died. I went to live with my grandmother in Los Angeles to keep her company. That gave me a chance to learn from her more about her life during WWII, during the Holocaust. She was very strong in her opinion about things that were not imaginable, things that she said nobody would ever know about, except those who went through the experience. She was glad that I was interested in talking with her and that I wanted to know more about the family that remained. There was family in Israel, family in Costa Rica, and family in France. Quite a few people came to my grandfather's funeral, and I made contact with them.

When I applied again for the Foreign Service, I flew to Washington for the tests; I again made it to the list, but my score was not quite enough to get in. I decided not to wait anymore in the United States but go to Israel and continue my studies there. Israel was the center of a lot of news focus, and I had family there. I thought it would be a good place to continue professionally, as I was interested in journalism and in a global perspective on events. This was 1982. I started in a kibbutz to study Hebrew and to get a better sense of society. It was Kibbutz Ein HaShofet. While there, I met a volunteer from Britain, and we became a couple there. Then she went back to her family in England, and I went to study communication at The Hebrew University in Jerusalem.

I studied the sociology of communication at the Master's level, how governments communicate with people; how different societies understand each other; the dynamics of different communication models. This was a fascinating environment and, while it may have been an Israeli perspective, most of the materials about mass communication were American. I had a disadvantage in that my Hebrew was rudimentary, but the materials were all in English and many of the lecturers were from the US and from Britain. I finished there in 1985. In the meantime, my girlfriend came back to Israel, also to study Hebrew and Judaism, and, at the end of 1985, we went to Britain and married there.

I started looking for work in Britain and thinking of applying again for the US Foreign Service. Eventually, I took up a research assistant position at City of London Polytechnic on new media, on government and communication towards a doctorate. It was a two-year program, but after one year, I was offered a position with the Foreign Service in 1987. I left the doctoral program and joined the Foreign Service. I had waited for this opportunity for a long time; also, I am an egalitarian at heart and degrees don't mean as much to me.

I joined the State Department in 1987 and came back to the US with my wife and first-born son who was born in 1986. Our second son was waiting to be born. We arrived in the US November 1987 and he was born in May 1988.

When you join the Foreign Service, there is an orientation program and my first assignment was going to Israel, which was fortuitous.

You requested it.

Yes. The accepted wisdom at the time was that if you have any previous experience, throw it away because you were going to be sent someplace else, about which you know nothing, but it was never the case with me. I knew the language and this position let me focus on my new career as a diplomat without having to also to learn all about the country of my assignment.

We arrived in the summer of 1988; I was a vice-consul for the first six months, adjudicating visa applications, and working with American citizens for the next six months. Then, I rotated into the political section, because we try to give our entry-level officers as extensive a range of experience as possible. In the political section, during my second year, I focused on Israel's relations with African countries, with international organizations, as well as with the diaspora Jewish communities, including some communities in the Middle-East.

This was from 1989 into 1990, and this was the fascinating time of regime change in many places. It was also the beginning of the large influx of Jews from Eastern Europe through Hungary and through other places. We tried to understand how the newcomers were integrating, and how this influx was changing Israeli society. For me, I was also able to focus on how to apply intercultural communication, communication between government and the public. Interviewing the persons applying for a visa. For me, as a consul, this was like a sociological experiment. I tried to understand their perspective from these short but informative interviews in which I was listening and engaging as much as just asking questions.

Our third child was born in Jerusalem while we were there.

The next assignment was New Delhi, after I studied Hindi for six months back in the US, bringing me up to a level to be able to have basic conversation.

Writing also?

Reading also. We have a five-point scale, zero to five. Zero is no proficiency at all; five is university-educated professional level fluency. Three is conversational fluency; with some flaws, but you can have a smooth conversation. Two is a working ability to have a professional conversation with mistakes, but you can still convey what you need to convey. I had a two for reading and two for speaking Hindi. I was in New Delhi from 1991 to 1993. I was interviewing people who wished to immigrate to the US. It was, again, a cultural experience. It was also an exercise in understanding how people met each other.

Were they spouses?

Many were. We normally think of marriage as a love relationship in the US and Western Europe, but that was not what was common in India. Love matches were frowned upon. What do people who are governed by their hormones know about each other? They can't think rationally; the relationship they happen to come across isn't going to last. It's better that their parents arrange the marriage for them; they think rationally, they know their children, and they know what's in the interest of their family. They can find the right person for their child to marry. That was the standard approach.

What was your task?

To understand whether their marriage was genuine, I asked them how they met.

What would be a wrong answer?

There is no wrong answer. In a conversation, you can see if things don't follow from one thing to another. Sometimes, for example, a person might claim to have fallen in love while studying in the US at a university; but during the interview it might become clear that the couple had never spoken to each other.

There have been films about such situations.

I've seen films, but I've also talked with real people; thousands of people,

Are those films realistic? I never knew the color of my wife's toothbrush.

Some elements in those films are realistic, but I don't like to play games with trick questions like the movies seem to portray. For me, it is a conversation; it's not a quiz. If a person is going to tell me about how they met their spouse, things either make sense in the conversation or they don't make sense in a conversation. We are not there to try to trick someone, but in a sustained conversation, there will be questions and clarifications. If the interviewee changes things too much, you can see that he or she is making something up. In the cases where there was deception, often it was that the person who was in the US had gone to the US when he had already married someone in India. In the US, the husband married an American without ever divorcing his Indian wife, in order to get a green card. Then, after getting his green card, he would divorce his American wife and apply for a visa for his original wife to come to the US.

Would, in such a situation, the American wife know that her marriage was a bogus one?

Hard to say; sometimes yes, sometimes, no. Sometimes, it was for money; sometimes, it wasn't. We had to sort out what actually happened as opposed to what people were telling us; this was my job. Trying to be courteous and professional, I was trying to have conversations that were direct. I was trying to understand the relationship.

In the case of a double marriage, for example, did you have the people involved prosecuted?

No, but it was grounds for not issuing a visa. The things that needed to be made clear were whether the person in the US had the right to apply for a visa for a family member to immigrate. If it turned out that the person in the US had obtained the green card by fraud, we would advise the Immigration and Naturalization Service, INS, as it was called at the time, of the circumstances and let them make the determination. If the status of the person was still valid, we would have to proceed. There was then the other question: whether the marriage between that person and his spouse was valid? But here I am merely emphasizing the importance of conversation between people of different cultures in trying to distinguish reality from what I am being told.

Did you like this job?

I liked these conversations. They gave me insight into the society and helped me in being able to discuss things with people, building rapport with people of a very different society.

During my time there, there was also the program of immigration of a thousand displaced Tibetans to the US. This program aimed at enhancing the understanding of the Tibetan situation. Congress had voted for a program to enable a thousand displaced Tibetans to immigrate to the US. Many Tibetans lived in India. The Dalai Lama was in India and I met with him. We discussed, among other things, how immigration affects people. When they come to the US, they bring their culture to the US, but it also changes them. One develops a strong internal sense of being American. Their children will be different from their immigrant parents just as I am different from my parents. This is regardless of where the family may have come from. Immigrants to the US take on the sense of being American very quickly, and their children, born and raised in the US, are generally raised knowing from childhood that, while their ethnic heritage may be different from that of their friends, they are fully American. The children of the Tibetans also, after a generation, will be providing a sense of the American situation back to the Tibetan culture overseas.

It is a very interesting societal dynamic—how immigration changes the immigrants and also changes the societies where they came from.

How do they change the society they are joining?

They increase our awareness of things that are happening around the world. It also enhances the understanding that America is a diverse society, made up of people from many different heritages.

What happened after India?

I spent one year back in the US studying Russian. We bought a house in Fredericksburg, Virginia, fifty miles south of Washington, because we wanted to have a place that our children could identify as our home. They were at a point when they were becoming aware of the world around them.

How intensive is such a course?

Five days a week, five hours a day, and there is homework as well. We also study the history, politics, and culture of the country. This was in 1993. It was already Russia and not the Soviet Union. The impression was that the revolution in telecommunication fostered the political changes in the world. We arrived in Moscow in 1994. I was in the consular section. The new shape of Russian society presented challenges, because international travel was no longer restricted. The old societal structure had crumbled where academics were close to the top of the elite; the top was the political elite, and high culture was the societal aspiration. Business people were not part of the old communist society. By the time we had arrived, the situation had changed, and business people, investors, entrepreneurs, people who could get money quickly were now stepping forward as the elite. The former elites in the arts, literature, and sciences, they now had a lower status; they had no money. The pensions of the elderly were worthless; there was confusion as they wondered, "What did we do all our lives? What had happened? What was our own history?" People could no longer believe anything they had been told before. There were a lot of scientists who wanted to emigrate.

Many did.

We had a program specifically geared toward Russian scientists, because we felt it was better if they came to the US rather than someplace else. We had to understand the new society in order to be able to offer consular services effectively. In the past many of those who had gotten out, wanted to stay in the US unless there was some need to come back. It was new that people could travel freely and would freely return to Russia. We could issue visitor visas only to people who had the intention to return. If the person wanted to immigrate to the US, there was a different process for that. Highly skilled scientists, for example, could immigrate easily and, as I said, we had a special program to facilitate their immigration. When people without special skills wanted to immigrate, we would have to explain to them that the process for an immigrant visa might be lengthy and more challenging than they had expected. US immigration law did not permit people who were likely to be a public charge, on welfare, to immigrate to the US.

However, we did have a diversity visa program, *the visa lottery*, as people call it. It highlights how much we value diversity in our society. Our immigration laws have changed over the years. Until 1965, our earlier immigration laws looked at the demographics of the US and said that x percent of the American population is of German origin; y percent is of British origin; z percent is of Indian origin; and so on. In order to maintain demographics based on country of origin, there was a quota system. In time, this was seen as unfair to countries whose citizens previously had not been able to come to the United States. It also limited our access to people with good job skills. We changed our laws in 1965 to focus more on family relationships and professional qualifications, while dropping the quota system altogether. We set a ceiling concerning the overall number of people who could immigrate into the US every year. The new regulations, however, had the unintended effect of favoring countries where there were large families and disadvantaging countries from which there were few immigrants in recent years. In favor of diversity, Congress established a new program, which looked at which countries had been disadvantaged by the changes in 1965 and offered immigrant visa opportunities to those countries not hitting the ceiling. This program offered visas to those countries by lottery for people that had the right educational level or professional qualifications. They needed to have at least a high school education or work experience in a profession that needed at least two years of training. At that level of education and training, they would probably find jobs in the US. It was good to see that in a country like Russia where so much of history contained anti-American sentiments, that is, under Soviet rule, so many were interested in immigrating through this diversity program. However, we had to be concerned about organized crime in Russia at the time and try to be sure that our visa policy was not being abused by people engaged in organized crime.

Was corruption considered?

Corruption was always a reason for ineligibility even when there was no special emphasis on it. Organized crime, which was the focus of our attention, often involves corruption. Moral turpitude has always been a consideration, which implied intention to commit a criminal act, or intention to deceive. Corruption is a crime of moral turpitude, but our law generally requires a conviction if commission of a crime of moral turpitude is the basis for the visa ineligibility.

Conviction where?

Any place. Conviction of a crime of moral turpitude, in countries where there was little accountability, little prospect that these people would be convicted, applying this law was harder. If there was no conviction, then generally the person must admit, under oath, that he committed a crime of moral turpitude. We were focusing on preventing people from using the visa process to engage in organized crime in the United States. However, this might mean that there was no conviction. Nevertheless, membership in an organized crime group was often enough to establish that the person was likely to engage in criminal activity in the US, and therefore, be ineligible for a visa. There were government officials who were linked to organized crime. There were government officials who were denied entry into the US because of their involvement in organized crime. Money laundering was among such crimes.

Did anybody try to bribe you?

I don't recall anybody trying to bribe us. What they might do was pay somebody who would claim that they would bribe someone. However, observing that these attempts at fraud took advantage of people's lack of information and general mistrust of government officials, I understood that we needed to be more transparent, explain our laws and explain our policies, and not be opaque. It was in the early days of the Internet and we created a website for the consular section and began putting information about applying for a visa on the website. We were one of the first embassies doing that. In the mid-1990s, it was up to the individual embassies to set up web sites.

Did you make friends in Moscow?

Yes.

Have you maintained your interactions?

For a little while afterwards, but not so much now.

How long did you stay in Moscow?

From 1993 to 1997. I came back to the US in 1997 for five years. We had our house in Fredericksburg; our children went to elementary school and to middle school, and we wanted them to live in American society for a while.

What were you doing for five years in the State Department?

For the first two years, I worked within our bureau of international organizations on conflict prevention. After the first gulf war, the UN Secretary General Boutros Boutros-Ghali announced his "Agenda for Peace" initiative. The idea was that we had managed to put together a huge, international coalition to fight against the aggression. This, however, had been a response to aggression rather than anticipating and preventing aggression. How could we work together in the future, not to just respond to a deadly conflict, but to prevent it? This was a question of developing preventive diplomacy.

Preventing conflict is much less costly than dealing with the aftermath of conflict. This was my portfolio for two years.

Then, I worked in the office of consular systems. Consular officers make their decisions about issuing visas based on information. I was posing the question, "what information do we need to have in order to make the right decision for the security of our country." We had to be courteous; we did not want to discuss issues in an information vacuum with somebody who wanted to come to the US. If the person is telling the truth, we should be able to understand that they are telling the truth, and be able to make informed decisions quickly. The consular systems office developed the technology that enabled us to have the information we needed to make informed decisions, and the automated processes we needed to issue visas and passports efficiently.

What was your next assignment?

In 2002, I went to Frankfurt to be a regional consular officer working with our small embassies in Africa. I was using the new technologies increasingly in sharing information with my colleagues, who were assigned to a number of different countries.

What was your level of seniority by then?

Our foreign service is structured with different grades. Six is the lowest level Foreign Service Officer grade, and that is the entry-level grade. Five is the next one up and four is the top of the entry-level ranks. The mid-level ranks are three, two, and one. In Frankfurt, I was a two, the middle of the mid-level ranks.

And now?

When I was in London, I was a one. After I got to Damascus, I entered the senior Foreign Service and had the rank of Counselor. Now, I have the rank of Minister Counselor.

Did you have this in Budapest?

Yes. The position in Budapest was for a person with the rank of Counselor, but shortly after I arrived, I was promoted to Minister Counselor. This is a personal rank. The system is similar to the military; regardless of the rank, there is the position.

What would be the next in ranks?

The next one is Career Minister, and the top is Career Ambassador.

Is there a retirement age?

The mandatory retirement age is 65.

In the US, generally, there is no mandatory retirement age.

In the Foreign Service, there is one. There are different criteria in the Foreign Service; if you are not promoted after certain period of time, then you are not able to remain in the service.

Is it a hint that you should resign?

You have to leave. It's an up or out system. You can't stay at the same level indefinitely; it's not like the civil service, or most other jobs, where you can remain in the same position indefinitely. In the Foreign Service, we change our jobs every three years, and we're also expected to advance in our careers, to show our potential and to rise. If you don't rise, then you can't remain in the service.

Your Budapest assignment was the highest in your career so far.

Yes. In each position, I'm in a higher grade. The Deputy Chief of Mission (DCM) serves multiple functions. It's second to the Ambassador.

The Ambassador not being a career diplomat is not expected to manage the embassy, so was your original assignment primarily managing the embassy?

Each section has a section head. The DCM is expected to keep them together and handle some of the management details of the embassy. We also have a management section that manages the efficient running of the machinery of the embassy.

For a statement, you probably have to be very careful, whereas in an interview, you have to be prompt.

When we issued our statements on the unveiling of the Horthy bust[13] or the statement on the monument on Szabadság tér,[14] it was a joint effort in the embassy and we coordinated with Washington, the State Department. In giving an interview, there is no possibility for consultation. You can see in these statements that we try to emphasize the common grounds between our ideals and the ideals that Hungary claims to have.

---

13 http://hungarian.hungary.usembassy.gov/pr_11072013.html
14 http://hungarian.hungary.usembassy.gov/pr_04222014.html

Statement of the United States Embassy in Budapest
regarding the unveiling of the bust of Horthy

November 7, 2013

The United States strongly condemns the shameful event organized by Jobbik, a Hungarian political party identified with ethnic hatred and anti-Semitism, to unveil a bust honoring Nazi ally Miklos Horthy, Hungary's leader during World War II, at the entrance to the Hungarian Reformed Church at the edge of Szabadsag tér in Budapest on November 3. Those who organized and participated in the event, including members of Hungary's Parliament, promoted not only their own intolerance, but also a dramatically negative image of Hungary. Although the significant number of counter-demonstrators showed there is strong opposition to the organizers' views, and members of the Hungarian government have expressed disapproval, an event such as this requires swift, decisive, unequivocal condemnation by Hungary's highest ranking leaders.

United States Embassy Statement Encouraging Dialogue

April 22, 2014

The United States has supported the desire of the Hungarian government and society to commemorate the events of 70 years ago when Nazi forces and their Hungarian allies rounded up and deported Hungarian Jews, Roma, and other minorities. We have, however, noted significant concerns raised within Hungarian society to government proposals related to this anniversary year, among them its plans for a new museum and a memorial to the "victims of the German occupation of Hungary." Hungarians from all walks of life, Jewish organizations, civil society groups and Hungary's international partners have expressed reservations about these plans.

The government had indicated in February it would resume dialogue after Easter with stakeholders concerned about Memorial Year plans. The government also communicated that it was postponing completion of the Memorial until the end of May 2014. Constructive engagement between a government and its citizens is a hallmark of good democratic governance, and we were encouraged by promises of dialogue. Following the government's election victory, genuine dialogue would demonstrate the government's commitment to discussing openly and transparently important issues even with those who may at times disagree with the government position.

As a fellow democracy, we continue to urge the government to seek an honest, open, and factual assessment of the Holocaust in Hungary. This includes soliciting and considering the opinions of all segments of Hungarian society, and especially those who are rightly most sensitive to the government's plans during this 70th anniversary year.

I was very impressed by your statement about the unveiling of the Horthy bust and our daughter even wrote a blog to respond to it.

I was involved, those who worked with me were involved, and we worked with Washington to have it as a formal statement that we could publish on behalf of the embassy. As regards interviews, speaking extemporaneously and being able to engage the public, this is something we have to be able to do and in this situation, you can't have every word you say be cleared. We have to know what our policies are; we have to be able to discuss our policies and engage effectively with others about our policies, and use a language that is suitable for the occasion.

Let's return to your story, your career, that is.

After Africa, we went to London in 2004. For this assignment, I didn't need a language course. Our oldest son graduated from high school in Frankfurt, and he'd chosen to go to university in Britain even before I was offered a position there. He was accepted at the University of Bath. Our two younger sons were in high school. We were living in the center of London; I was heading the American citizen services section within a large consular section with about a hundred employees. In the American citizen services section, we had about forty employees. There were about a quarter of a million Americans living in Britain. There were many support systems for the Americans living there, and I wanted to make sure that the embassy was an active member of that support system, taking on a leadership role. We wanted it to be more than something people could turn to in emergency, but rather be seen as an integral part of their lives.

What happened after London?

I went back to the US in 2008 to study Arabic. By now, all our sons were at university. Thus, I could go someplace even where there might be safety problems, but with our sons away, we wouldn't have to worry about that. I was ready to go anyplace. The plan was for me to study Arabic for one year in Washington and the second year in Tunis, and then go to Damascus for two years of service.

Not three years?

The normal assignment is three years, but in dangerous or unusually difficult places, two years. My wife did not want to travel so much anymore, and the plan was that she would stay in London where she had a job. After I began studying Arabic, the Syrians were upset with the Americans, because of what they alleged was an American attack on Syrian territory. There was a convoy providing support for terrorist activity in Iraq and the convoy was attacked. The Syrians closed the American school at the embassy, and they closed the American cultural center in Damascus. The embassy families with children had to send their children away. My predecessor in Damascus had children; his wife and children left, and he wanted to leave as well, but could not until I got there. I thus went to Syria after just one year of Arabic language training and arrived in Damascus in 2009. Now, this meant less traveling and there was also a job opportunity at the embassy, my wife joined me. It was an enjoyable country to be in. It was a police state, so it was safe, as long as you didn't engage in political activity. It was so pleasant that we decided to extend our stay to three years according to which we would have been leaving in the middle of 2012. However, the Arab Spring started in December 2010. It gradually engulfed the region, and it changed our plans. Family members of the embassy had to leave in April 2011 and the rest of us left, not all at once, but we were all gone by February 2012.

After a few months upon my return to Washington, I began studying Hungarian. My wife had been back in Washington since April 2011, and we prepared for our arrival in Budapest. Coming to Budapest, my focus would be on effective management of the embassy team; in some ways, looking more internally. I wanted to make sure that the different sections of the embassy worked together cooperatively; they shared information with each other.

This was a new type of task for you, different from consular work.

Yes, although in Damascus I was the second highest-ranking person in the embassy. There was no ambassador; the deputy chief of mission was the Chargé there, and when he was away, I was the Chargé d'Affaires. My philosophy has always been that we had to work together as a team. Budapest was an opportunity to bring all the sections together, roughly a hundred

Americans and over two hundred Hungarians at the embassy. This is how it is in many embassies, more local employees than Americans.

When I arrived in Budapest in August 2013, we did not have an ambassador, but I thought that there was going to be an ambassador fairly soon; I thought that my focus would be on the internal workings of the embassy. As I knew that at least for a short time I would be in charge of the embassy, I spoke with the people at the Hungarian embassy in Washington. I spoke with one adviser to the Prime Minister and several other members of the Hungarian government before coming to Hungary. In talking with them, I wanted to make it clear that I am aware of what the media says and of the polarized perspectives, but I believed in direct observation and in not making up my mind until I see things with my own eyes.

It is important for me and for the embassy to speak with all sides; speak with the government, speak with the opposition, and speak with civil society, to hear all the different perspectives, and for us to be able to make informed decisions. This means not to rely on what the press says or what the government says, but to take a broader approach, to be confident that what we are seeing and hearing is a good foundation to be able to advise Washington about what's going on. After my arrival, I met with members of government, with civil society members, just as every senior person at an embassy does. I tried to attend events where I was invited by people of all sides. When we were still waiting for the ambassador, I tried not to have a prominent public role, but as more time went by, we could not remain silent simply because we had no ambassador. Things began happening; the unveiling of the Horthy bust, where we felt it was important to highlight our perspective of shared values. It was a matter of how we view hate speech, how important it is for people in authority to speak out against hatred.

Have you ever visited the Museum of Military History in Buda?

Yes, and you have in mind the Horthy memorial there.

Yes.

For us, it was not an issue of Horthy; it was an issue of context. What we spoke about in that statement was the context in which this bust was now publicized. The bust had already been there previously, existing inside the church, but now it was moved out to make it more publicly visible. Horthy was being used by Jobbik, by those who supported a revisionist view of history, to try to rehabilitate, to present Hungary's Nazi-ally leader in a way that diminished his role. They presented this view of Hungary as an expansionist, ethnic nation, and alienated those parts of the population that suffered under Horthy's rule. This context, in which it was being presented, should be addressed. The divisive speech had to be addressed, to address the use of Horthy to spread hatred towards other Hungarian citizens. We spoke out then. It was still a statement and not a conversation with the public. We put out a message and heard the reaction.

People thought it was good that the embassy had said something, but nothing changed. After that, we continued to try to engage the government on a number of bilateral issues, societal issues. There were tensions between the government and particularly the Jewish community with regards to the way the Holocaust commemoration year was being approached, with regards to anti-Semitism, with regards to the curriculum.

These issues appeared to be moving forward well, but by the end of December 2013, the government announced quietly that it would construct a monument on Szabadság tér, which raised a lot of concern because many Hungarians interpreted the monument as a disavowal of Hungarian responsibility for the Holocaust and implied that Hungary was a victim of the Germans. We didn't enter this discussion about Hungarian history. Throughout this period, we talked with the government about things that the government could do to address the concerns that the public had. We had regular contacts with the different ministries and were part, for example, of János Lázár's panel dealing with the Holocaust commemoration. Every week, nearly every day, we would meet with someone from the Hungarian government, one or another member of our embassy, and I would meet with someone from the government maybe twice a week or so. There was a lot of engagement on a variety of issues, be it the curriculum in the schools or something else. We were trying to see how we could work together to move forward in areas of common interest. The Hungarian government wanted to show what it was doing to address anti-Semitism, to address the concerns about democracy, about civil society. And we were prepared to tell the Hungarian government how their approach would be perceived in the US. We would also tell them what we might be able to do to help them in their efforts. We told them how we could help them with the curriculum, or try to see what the progress is with the curriculum so that we could express encouragement, or express some concern about delay. There were initiatives that the Hungarian government had committed to, that they were addressing. The curriculum was one; another was an increase in visits by schoolchildren to the Holocaust Museum. In some other areas, they were not moving so quickly, and in yet some other areas, we differed in our interpretation. Concerning our public communications, we did not think it was fruitful to make statements; one statement after the other. If we are there to engage with the government with a common vision, it doesn't help to have arguments in public. Usually, when I was speaking in public, I was trying to highlight where we might work together, but I know that it was often taken as criticism.

In what way?

We made statements about the Horthy bust and hate speech in October 2013 and one about the monument and the need for engagement with society on contentious issues in April 2014, right after the elections. It was when the construction began. When the audits of civil society organizations happened, we had to ask, how do we approach this area of common concern? In a democracy, it is important to have an engaged civil society, and with this, getting back to the open government commitments. Working with civil society is one of those commitments. Engaging with citizens in a constructive partnership; that's an aspect of open government. It was also for which there was a Hungarian commitment, too. In this case, another statement by the embassy might not have been the best way to approach it. This was something of a more general concern. There were organizations where these values were of the primary focus. This was part of transparency and good governance. This is why the next statement, the one about the intimidation of civil society and the media was not from the embassy but from the Organization for Security and Co-operation in Europe (OSCE). At the same time, I had to ask, how can we have a real conversation with the public? Not just to have a statement that comes and goes, but a real conversation? I had been out, talking with people, with different groups, but I wanted to engage in an ongoing conversation. This was something that I thought was really important here. What is the mood of the Hungarian people? It's hard to understand how the society feels if your door is not open to talk with them. I was looking for ways that would allow me to have such interactions, not through statements, but in a dialog.

I started a blog in January 2014, but that didn't lead to a lot of discussion. Even though I was raising issues of discussion in the US, I was hoping that the discussion would move to issues in Hungary. I could talk about the forced integration of our school system in the late 1950s. It was clearly a domestic US matter with reference to the law about separate but equal education, in which you create separate facilities, which are theoretically equal. That was what the Supreme Court decided. Treating everyone equally by creating separate communities, for us in the US, inevitably led to favoring the majority community. It is truly impossible to provide minority communities equal services. Eventually, in order to ensure equality, we integrated our communities. It was a difficult thing to do; there were riots, there were protests, but it brought about a huge change in our society to say that we can only have equality when we are all participating together. This is truly a discussion about American society and the people I was talking to about it might have not been familiar with *Brown versus the Kansas Board of Education*.[15] But people reacted, and some said, that might work in America, but it won't work here. So, let's have a discussion, why wouldn't it work here? How do you deal with the principle of equality when resources are not able to adequately provide equal opportunities?

We are far from "separate but equal" conditions: The Prime Minister's comment about the gypsies (Roma) and his reference to them as a crisis of migrants viewed in comparison to the current immigration problem and the manner in which authorities are considering this matter—this demonstrates how far we are from a reasonable approach concerning this matter.

For me, just saying, "isn't the Prime Minister's stand on this issue outrageous", would not help finding the way to solving this problem. My saying, "Here is our experience in the US. This is our perspective on these societal issues." Even without me making a direct connection, people can recognize

---

15   *Brown v. Board of Education of Topeka*, 347 U.S. 483 (1954).

the existence of these issues in their country, too. I can talk about why we have the values we have and that our values are shared values. I can talk about our belief in equality and about our belief of treating all our citizens with fairness.

My impression has been that the US administrations were always in the forefront of progress in such matters.

That may be your perspective, but in reality, civil society pushed the government to the forefront of progress, but it took a lot of effort.

What do you do these days?

I am working on our Open Government plans of the State Department for 2016. I'm trying to shape our policy and also identify what it is that we are doing. We are a large organization and having been away from Washington for many years, this deep involvement in the State Department's internal processes helps me understand and shape the Department's decision-making processes. Sometimes one office may not know what another one is doing. I am working on what we in the State Department are doing for Open Government, and how can we leverage the things we are doing now to highlight the best practices and to best shape the direction where we are going.

Is this kind of office work a letdown after your activities in Budapest?

It's not a let-down; it's different. There is always some apprehension coming back to Washington. Embassy life is very different. There you are in a smaller, manageable community, especially if you are in charge of the mission, and you have a great degree of flexibility in what you are doing. Back in Washington, the work environment is more complex. The challenge now is to understand the maze of our bureaucracy, and it's a different challenge.

Looking back at all your assignments, does Hungary stand out in any way?

With each assignment, there was increased responsibility and there was something unexpected in Hungary in that I arrived with something in mind, to be deputy chief, and I became the chief, and it was not what I expected. My engagement with the public was so successful and generated such an immense response. There were far more people interested in engaging on platforms such as Twitter than was anticipated. The mainstream media, the press, Internet portals, followed what was on the social media and carried it over to the mainstream media. This generated a large-scale conversation among the Hungarian public on the issues of open government, transparency, corruption, accountability. This was more than anybody anticipated.

Did the thought ever occur to you of running for office in Hungary?

In Hungary? [Heartily laughing] I know that people were joking about that. There were web sites set up to promote me for Prime Minister. In many ways, it highlighted my interests in addressing various issues in the United States. In Hungary, I talked about shared values and about the need to work together, but trying carefully to not directly involve myself in a conversation about Hungarian governance. Back in the United States, I can directly involve myself in that type of conversation.

You have tried to convince me that there was nothing extraordinary in what you did in Hungary.

I did not try to get involved in directly discussing Hungarian internal affairs. However, as far as innovation, taking more advantage of the available communication technologies, I know that I did something different from my predecessors and different from many of my colleagues. It was not unique though.

I think it was, and you had an unprecedented impact as far as the activities of diplomats are concerned in recent times. When previously I asked if your superiors are aware of what you did and with what results, your response was, "Not quite."

The value of how we manage these multiple conversations that are taking place, how we engage in them, what impact it has, whether you build a rapport, that is seen as very difficult to manage and to institutionalize. You and

I were talking earlier about the change in the world since 1965 [IH's first interview recording; this is a reference to a previous conversation]. At that time, certainties existed; there was a clear-cut approach of "us and them," there was the ability to control the relations between the superpowers, and we could understand what was going on in that world. We seemed to be moving in a structured, orderly manner towards the future. In contrast, now, when life is better and freer, but when there are so many different currents, so many different things happening; there are risks that are difficult to assess and address. So many people can get onto the Internet and influence others. Changes are happening so rapidly that is difficult to follow, let alone to plan ahead and have a strategy to implement and keep to it over a period of time and see how things develop. This is part of the value and part of the fear with regard to the power in these conversations.

Your activities in Hungary helped Hungarian society in generating discussions of important issues, enhancing the belief that it is worth to keep these discussions going. Your activities and the conversations they generated held a mirror in front of many of us to see ourselves in perspective. Your activities also helped the United States in projecting an image that people who like to think for themselves find attractive; they brought the United States closer to people; they showed the United States through a human being who made the effort to understand and who appeared to care.

The main theme that we must not forget was open government, transparency, collaboration; this is what my activities were about. I wanted to open our doors to the public and humanize our efforts.

Then, it was a fortunate coincidence of policy goals and the individual who happened to be there implementing them.

Why fortunate coincidence? It is a challenge to practice open government. We don't all do it. We don't all feel comfortable engaging with civil society, with private citizens, and speaking openly about what we are doing. What I was trying to do in Budapest, I had tried doing in every post I had had.

The circumstances in Budapest lent emphasis to your efforts.

My approach was the same everywhere.

But not the outcome. Are you maintaining any ties with Hungary?

I'm talking to you. [Laughing] I still have a number of friends there, and they are close to my heart. I maintain quite a few ties. Hungary is a microcosm of many of the issues that affect us all, governance, national identity, our role in the world, the role of civil society, so many of these things. I try to maintain strong ties.

Do you have a dream-next-assignment?

[Pause] I try to make each assignment a dream. Each place is not what I'd expected; Budapest itself was not what I'd expected. I knew my own capabilities and I adapted my role, and turned this assignment into something that reflected what I could offer. I did the same in Damascus and in London; what I step into and the way I approach it is never going to be the same as my predecessor might have done.

My question was like when they ask an opera singer, you have sung in many roles; what is your dream role?

It's hard, because there are going to be places where I would love to serve. I am not going to name them, because if I get it, great, if I don't, I don't want you to feel sorry for me. Concerning the actual nature of the assignment, and I may not want to advertise this, but I was never sure if I wanted to be an ambassador. I have mentioned to you that I am an egalitarian at heart. I don't like all the extra attention and focus that comes just because of a title. Being able to accomplish great things while being without the advantage of a title, but by virtue of doing it, that is what appeals to me. Whatever my next assignment will be, and it may look modest at start, it can be made into a very valuable opportunity.

Meeting with "Martians"[16]

At some point, as if for relaxation, I suggested that we consider a few of the statements made by those famous Hungarian-American scientists who are known collectively as "the Martians of Science," and see André's quick responses to them. What makes the statements of the Martians especially interesting in the present context is that they could see American and world affairs from the perspectives of their Hungarian backgrounds. The Martians' statements (printed in a different font to distinguish them) were made many decades ago, yet they appear to have contemporary relevance.

JOHN VON NEUMANN, "I never found a 'compromise' [with Nazi Germany] possible neither desirable."

Compromising with something as evil as that, I agree would not have been possible nor desirable. If Nazi Germany kept to the principles that it was espousing, then, what kind of compromise would be possible? You can't compromise with a country that is determined to eradicate its population.

Some countries have pledged to eradicate Israel. Would any compromise be possible with such countries?

Compromise is not giving up something and saying, "OK, We'll live with you. You do what you want and we do what we want, and we'll work

---

16   For the sources of all the quotes, see Balazs Hargittai and Istvan Hargittai, *Wisdom of the Martians of Science: In Their Own Words with Commentaries* (World Scientific 2016).

together." Compromise is an agreement in which each side changes something as opposed to simple co-existence; the existing behavior continuing. A big part of diplomacy is to try to apply peaceful means to eliminate that behavior which is detrimental to society; to find a way in which we can preserve our values and live together peacefully. One way to put it is to say to Nazi Germany, "If you give up"—it is so hard even to envisage, because it was so central to what they were about—"if you give up the core values that this Aryan supremacy philosophy holds, if you accept that all citizens in Germany are equal citizens and that human rights should be valued with regards to freedom of speech and the ability to worship as you choose, that all people are equal regardless of race or ethnicity, or religion, then, OK, we can talk."

At that time, in the late 1930s, the main problem of the democracies with Nazi Germany was not human rights violations. The problem was Germany's aggression against one country after another. The most conspicuous compromise with Nazi Germany was the Munich Agreement in which the United Kingdom just fooled itself while selling out Czechoslovakia for the sake of a "compromise" with Germany.

We are not necessarily disagreeing. Apart from pure aggression, the military action was not just an irrational, random act. There was a stated cause. They wanted the territories on which the ethnic German nationals were living.

That was the pretext.

That was the pretext. If you say, you cannot use that pretext, that there are political states that exist and the citizens in those states are the citizens of those states and neighboring state do not have a claim towards the territory of the ethnic group that lives there. Then, there is no basis for the military expansion.

Hitler said, once we add this piece of Czechoslovakia, we'll have no more demands, and, of course, he did not mean to keep his word.

But what justified his initial claim in the first place?

Whatever justified it, the western powers accepted it as part of the Munich Agreement.

We can look back with hindsight and say that it did not prevent anything.

In this case, we don't need the benefit of hindsight. Winston Churchill saw it then and there that it was not going to accomplish anything.

Let's say that if Germany were seeking that territory because that territory had contained its capital and they had been forced to move their capital to a temporary location; furthermore, the only source of income for the economy was the coal or the oil in that territory and they needed that territory both for historical integrity and for their survival as a political state; if they could say that that territory had been taken from them because that neighboring country had beaten them and had taken it from them, then, there is no ideological reason not to compromise, not to work on some type of solution. A country trying to change state boundaries and willing to enter negotiations in order to change state boundaries with a rational cause; why not try to work on trying to find a solution on that? Here, the basis for that territorial claim was one that could never be satisfied. The claim that we want all the territory on which our ethnic group resides is not an acceptable cause. What happens when the ethnic group grows? Do you now have a right to claim that additional territory? My focus on this hypothetical question is on the challenges and the difficulty in using ethnicity as the basis for forming a state. That's a very complex discussion. The reprehensible part of Nazi philosophy was this sense that: "there are different types of human populations—some of which are subhuman and that they are not valued citizens of our state and we have the right as the superior human group to eliminate the inferior human group."

Discussing the situation with Nazi Germany and the Munich Agreement, the question comes to mind: how is it possible for the United States to come to an agreement with Iran without Iran abandoning its "Death to America" determination, let alone its commitment to annihilate Israel? It is well known that Iran sponsors terrorist activities world-wide and the agreement will free enormous sums for Iran that can further such activi-

ties. We are talking about an amount of money in the order of magnitude of a hundred billion dollars.

We are trying to find a way forward. How do we not try to work towards something that will lead to a more stable region? Do we just ignore Iran and pretend that things will get better if we don't engage and the only solution is to use military force? What we try to do is maintain our military strength so that we can address any military issue that can arise. At the same time, we have to be able to work for a peaceful solution. The agreement that we have come to has to be reviewed, but if it meets the criteria to be a positive way forward, why not do that?

However, you have eloquently explained to me why it is impossible to come to a compromise with a power that does not give up certain basic tenets; in this case they include Death to America and the annihilation of Israel, not to speak about terrorist activities, and not even letting American prisoners to go.

There are basic ideologies that would be difficult to compromise with. We have discussed the case of Nazi Germany.

Now we are discussing Iran.

I don't want to go into an analysis of Iran's ideologies now, but I don't know that they have the same world view as the Nazis. When they use the slogan "Death to America," that does not mean that they hold a world-view of being superior and they really intend to wipe out the United States. In order for them to change their policies, you have to negotiate with them. We are getting far from open government. These are the things that the negotiators would be discussing.

Are they still discussing it?

They have come up with a framework that they have put forward now. You know that the Iran agreement has been very much a matter of discussion over the past few weeks. It's still a matter of discussion. People are looking at the details; what does it offer what does it not offer?

There are one hundred senators of whom the support of 40 senators would suffice for the president to go ahead with the agreement. That means to me that the senators representing a great majority of Americans would be opposing the agreement, yet it would be concluded. Do I understand this correctly? This would be a very poor victory for the president.

But it is a victory. The fact is that in this environment where there is so much polarizing discussion and where the Senate is split as much as it is, and where the House [of Representatives] and where society are split as much as they are, then the president is still able to pull that number, it's worth moving forward.

JOHN VON NEUMANN in 1941. "The present war against Hitlerism is not a foreign war...,"

This is a discussion of values that affect us all. This is not simply about territory. This is not the case of one country simply seeking to expand into another; it is not a conflict between just two countries. This was a battle between values.

So it was not a foreign war.

No, it wasn't. The values they represented would have reshaped Europe and would have changed the values that we had subscribed to. It would have made it difficult for any country in the world to be able to subscribe to the values of equality. This is also why in the United Nations the Universal Declaration of Human Rights is based on values that we all subscribe to.

Both VON NEUMANN and THEODORE VON KÁRMÁN liked to say, "only a man from Budapest can enter a revolving door behind you and emerge ahead of you."

[Laughing] Every country has its unique attributes. I don't know if that is one of the unique attributes of Budapest.

THEODORE VON KÁRMÁN, "Only through openness of thought can good minds nourish one another and make contributions to mankind."

That ties in very much with what we were just talking about.

Yet Soviet scientists did make important discoveries even under their iso-lated conditions and under the repressive regime they worked.

Think of how much more they could have accomplished if they had been able to communicate freely with the rest of the world.

LEO SZILARD, "The salvation of the United States can come only from political sagacity."

Yes, we need wisdom.

You have it?

We aspire to it and we need to be told when we are not showing it.

LEO SZILARD, "In Washington, policy is made by those who operate rather than by those who are engaged in policy planning."

That is changing with more communication between those who plan and those who operate as we try to share information more effectively with each other. In the past, it was more difficult for the closed environment in Washington to know what was happening in the field. Policy had to catch up with events after they were taking place. Now, there is much more communication. What we need to do is to avoid paralysis. This refers back to what we were talking about with regard to the hierarchical system and the more flexible system. When you introduce the new technologies of better communication into our system, if people in the policy offices are able to directly affect what's happening in the field, it could lead to paralysis. People in the field and in the mid-level won't feel free to operate as effectively as before.

LEO SZILARD, "... Americans were free to say what they think, because they did not think what they were not free to say."

[Laughing] It's positive that we say what we actually feel. We are saying what we actually believe.

LEO SZILARD, "Just how free a man is to say what he thinks in an international meeting depends not only from what nation he comes, but also how closely he works with his own government."

This may apply to you as a diplomat and you don't need to comment.

I like to comment. If we are a nation that's able to say what we believe and that has internalized the values that we espouse, then we are able to speak freely wherever we are. This concerns institutionalizing values as opposed to the situation of Raoul Wallenberg or Carl Lutz, people who did the right thing, but had to go against their governments' policies. Of course, the Swedes supported much of what Wallenberg actually did although he went beyond his mandate. Lutz was more constrained.

Actually, Szilard's statement reflected his experience of the Pugwash meetings where East and West met and where private citizens free of government interference came from the West and intellectuals carefully selected and controlled by the government came from the Soviet Union. The next is a Szilard story referring to the American-Soviet stalemate in the issue of nuclear weaponry. He raised the question of what it might entail if they stopped hurting each other at a certain point while exercising the concept of MAD (mutually assured destruction). In Szilard's story, Joe and Tom are walking down the road. Joe offers twenty dollars to Tom if Tom swallows a toad. Tom does that however repellent it is. Joe regrets the loss of his twenty dollars and when Tom offers him twenty dollars if he swallows a toad, he does that. They continue their walk, their purses intact in the final account, but each richer with a most repellent experience.

I was expecting that swallowing a toad they would end up dead at the end of their walk. [Laughing]

Don't you think that building up such an arsenal of terrible nuclear arms acted as a mutual deterrence and did save the world from a third world war?

It also made it possible that a world war could be triggered.

Yes, but it didn't.

It didn't. It's hard to know whether it was the policy of mutually assured destruction that prevented that or the stand-off during the Cuban missile crisis, but it still required two people to stare each other down and know that one was just as strong as the other.

That was the policy of MAD, exactly.

I know. It was a big risk and we made our way through. Now we will have ideologically-based fighters who may also have these capabilities. What happens when the other side is not thinking rationally?

It is already the situation when it is not two great powers facing each other, but the West facing irrational forces.

That's a shift from one situation where there is just the two of us and we know each other to one where we can't be sure that this arsenal will have the same effect that we had thought. What do we do when we don't know who the enemy is and we are being attacked?

Again, Szilard wondered why the Germans so easily succumbed to Hitler and the Nazis.

People want to feel that they are better. What's his answer?

Szilard concluded that it was because they had a utilitarian approach:

"...the Germans always took a utilitarian point of view. They asked, Well, suppose I would oppose this, what good would I do? I wouldn't do very much good, I would just lose my influence. Then why should I oppose it? ... the moral point of view was completely absent ..."

In some ways, it resembles the happenings of the past five years in Hungary when separate segments of society are hurt and the protests come from those segments of society, but not generally.

This reminds me of that quote,

> "First they came for the Socialists, and I did not speak out—
> Because I was not a Socialist.
> Then they came for the Trade Unionists, and I did not speak out—
> Because I was not a Trade Unionist.
> Then they came for the Jews, and I did not speak out—
> Because I was not a Jew.
> Then they came for me—and there was no one left to speak for me."[17]

There is an exhibit now on at the Holocaust Museum in Washington on bystanders; it has been on for over a year. It shows the role of those who were complacent and just watched what happened—facilitating the events.

EUGENE P. WIGNER, "... decision can be wise only if the citizen is well-informed."

This is exactly what you have elaborated on, so I am not going to ask for your reaction.

EUGENE P. WIGNER, "The magic of democracy is that it never depends too much on any one man."

Again, I think, we can let this one go without a specific response.

---

17 Martin Niemöller (1892–1984) was a prominent Protestant pastor who emerged as an outspoken public foe of Adolf Hitler and spent the last seven years of Nazi rule in concentration camps. See, for example, https://encyclopedia.ushmm.org/content/en/article/martin-niemoeller-first-they-came-for-the-socialists

Edward Teller, "Opposing a program might be done not by presenting the perspectives and facts that argue against an issue, but by attempting to undermine the credibility of the people who are arguing for it."

Attack the man, not the idea.

Edward Teller, "In America, one is expected to tell the truth."

This is less trivial than it sounds.

I realize that. This gets to what I had been talking about before when countering fraud. We try to explain things in such a way that people trust us; that they feel that they are getting a truthful answer from us. My experience was that with regards to what people felt when speaking to a government official, that they should lie, and expected that no government official was going to tell them the truth. Coming from the American environment, telling the truth is an important way to actually get the result that you're looking for. In a democracy though, we expect that our politicians lie, but we also expect them to tell the truth. This is getting back to what I'd said before that taking what a government says it will do as fact, but then holding it to it, holding government accountable. This is as opposed to saying that we know that they are lying, so we can't pay attention to what they are saying because whatever they say does not matter, because they are going to do something else. Instead, having it as the expectation that governments will tell the truth, and the citizens have the responsibility to hold the governments accountable. That is one of the basic principles that we are looking for in open government. The citizens need to be engaged, they need to know that government actions conform to government words. Even when it is not the cultural practice in the place to tell the truth, transparency helps to change that cultural practice. There is an expectation that you will tell the truth, that you'll be held accountable to what you say. It may be that the next generation will expect that, yes, this is the norm and that there is no advantage to lying; in fact, there is a disadvantage. In democracy, without the right information, how can citizens be informed, how can citizens hold their elected officials accountable?

Edward Teller, "In a democracy we say that powers should be divided."

This requires no comment.

EDWARD TELLER, "When the actions in one country influence what happens in another country, then complete national independence is gone."

Being a member in the EU obviously means giving up some part of independence.

Being a part of any organization requires that we work as a member of that organization. If you are member of any group or social club, you are expected to follow the norms of that group even if you might feel differently.

Or get out.

Yes, leave it, but it's very hard to leave the world.

EDWARD TELLER, "It will not be easy to introduce freedom and respect for the individual in those parts of the world where these ideas never have yet taken root."

It's hard to introduce foreign ideas, but in most places, there is a desire to have freedom. How do you understand the concept of freedom? We have talked about the concept of freedom versus anarchy. It is hard, but not impossible.

EDWARD TELLER, "History is full of examples, how one little action can change the course of history."

Not in a democracy though.

Now with this rise of a *zeitgeist*, of a meme, of an action that stirs people and can reverberate. I'm thinking about Rosa Park's refusing to get from her seat on a bus.

It had tremendous consequences, but do you think her action was a disturbance of democracy; we should rather interpret it as an action towards a more complete democracy.

I'm thinking of the assassination of a president.

Of course, it was not a "little" action; rather, a big one. Yet even that action did not change the course of history; if anything, what happened, the smooth transition of presidential power demonstrated the stability, rather than the instability, of the democratic system.

EDWARD TELLER, "A dictatorship can use secrecy as a weapon. The weapon of democracy should be openness."

This is exactly what we were talking about.

How did you feel about Edward Teller?

Our politics may have been different, but we both were fighting for democracy.

Photos

André Goodfriend, fall 2015, at the Hungarian Consulate General, New York.
Photograph by Istvan Hargittai.

After returning to the U.S. in 2015, I enjoyed the opportunities that arose to travel to New York from time to time, to attend a presentation or meet with a friend. I'd read your book, "Budapest Scientific" and was fascinated by your interpretation of Hungary's historical memory through its public statues. So, I was particularly happy to be here, among friends, to explore the public stories we tell. The stories we tell through our statues give an implicit context to our environment. We can't help but see them, even though we may overlook them and only acknowledge them subconsciously. In this particular photo I note that I'm wearing a necktie that might have generated comment in the Hungarian media for the messages possibly hidden in its patterns. I hope that these pages highlight that openness is often much more productive than secrecy.

Istvan Hargittai (left) and André Goodfriend during their conversations, fall 2015, in Pennsylvania.

Photograph by and courtesy of Magdolna Hargittai.

A theme of this book is the importance of conversation, and this photo captures us as we settle in to talk. The weather was pleasant and the air clear. I had enjoyed the drive from Washington, DC, and looked forward to strengthening our acquaintanceship through conversation The only thing missing in the photo is the coffee.

André Goodfriend and the Dalai Lama, 1993, in India.

From André Goodfriend's Archives.

At the end of November 1990, several months before I arrived in New Delhi as a Vice Consul in February 1991, President George H.W. Bush signed the Immigration Act of 1990 into law. Among its provisions was the creation of a program to issue immigrant visas to 1,000 "displaced Tibetans" living in India, Nepal or Bhutan. The program was set to begin in October 1991. The criteria for the program were challenging. Visa recipients had to show that they were not already successfully resettled, but that they had the potential to be resettled successfully in the U.S. In order for the 1,000 visas to have the biggest impact, visa applicants were choosing to leave family, their spouses and children, behind with the prospect of applying for their family members to join them in the US later, but not as part of the program. Coordinating closely with Washington and with the Central Tibetan Administration (CTA) in Dharamshala, India, we established a process that made it possible to implement the program successfully, issuing all 1,000 visas within the mandated two years.

In the Spring of 1993, after the program had been in place for about a year and a half, I traveled to Dharamshala with my family to get a sense of the program from the Tibetan perspective and to meet with the Dalai Lama, who, at the time, was both a spiritual leader as well as the political head of the CTA.

We discussed the hopes for the "Displaced Tibetan" program as well as the nature of nationhood. On the one hand, a more global Tibetan diaspora would increase awareness of the plight of Tibetans without an independent political state; while on the other hand, generations born in the US to parents who have successfully resettled in the US, may have a different perspective and identity than those who had not immigrated to the US. It was a conversation that resonates throughout many discussions of ethnic heritage and national identity.

André Goodfriend in Palmyra, Syria, 2011. Many of these historic places have since been reported as looted, damaged or destroyed, either by the Islamic State or others with little respect for the multi-hued fabric of history.
From André Goodfriend's Archives.

Many diplomats, tourists and residents of Syria and the region were awed, like I was, by the complex history conveyed in the stones that shaped the still-living cities or that stood as ruined reminders in the desert of the civilizations that had shaped the region. These diverse threads continued to live within Syrian society while I was there, whether in the Aramaic-speaking Christians whose beliefs were considered heresy by the Byzantines, or the ruling Alawites, or the majority Sunni, or the increasing Shi'a, or the Druze, Yazidis, Kurds, Circassians, Jews, Armenians and others who all made up the peoples of Syria.

Palmyra signifies a past of global significance that is little-known outside Syria. For a couple years, in the second half of the third century CE, Palmyra was the capital of an empire that had taken over much of the eastern Roman Empire, from Egypt to Ankara. Perhaps emblematic of how we can lose touch with our past, I once spoke with a family where the mother was from a rural area and spoke only Aramaic; one daughter, who had remained with the mother spoke Aramaic and Arabic while the other daughter had moved away to the city and forgotten the Aramaic of her childhood and could no longer easily converse with her mother except through her sister as an intermediary.

André Goodfriend with Senator John McCain (left), 2014, in Budapest.

Photograph taken by the embassy photographer.

Both Senator McCain and I were closely connected with Arizona. I'd grown up there and McCain represented Arizona in the Senate. Our time in Arizona did not, however overlap. I had moved away from Arizona at the beginning of the 1980s, shortly before McCain arrived in the state. Over the decades, McCain had come to epitomize the independent streak which many Arizonans like to think is a part of their desert-hewn character. In January, 2014, Senator McCain of Arizona led a Congressional delegation to Hungary where they met with a range of political figures as well as with Prime Minister Orbán. There may have been an expectation that McCain would show support for the populist, conservative realpolitik being pursued by the Prime Minister, perhaps again demonstrating his independent streak, but this was not the case. In this photo, McCain and I are on our way to the venue of the delegation's press conference where, among other things, he noted the seriousness of the "concerns about the state of democracy in Hungary that have been raised by people both inside and outside of this country."

André Goodfriend participating in the "March of the Living."

From André Goodfriend's Archives.

There is something special and emotionally moving to join with others in celebrating that, despite efforts to murder our grandparents and parents, we have survived and we are here, proud of our role in moving civilization away, even a little bit, from this state-sponsored, institutionalized savagery.

My father's parents were born in Poland. Entire branches of my family were murdered during the Holocaust because they were Jewish. My grandfather didn't speak much about what he endured during WWII, except that he had been interred in a French POW camp. My grandmother, on the other hand, while saying that no one would ever understand what they had gone through, described her childhood in a religious household in Bialystok, how the relatives and friends of her youth had been killed, and how she and my five-year-old father, evaded the Nazis in southern France.

In this photo, taken during the 2014 March of the Living, I am standing next to the Polish Ambassador Roman Kowalski. A hundred years earlier, our grandparents were children living perhaps 100 miles apart. Thirty years later, xenophobia, ethnic nationalism and populist authoritarianism had destroyed the world around them. And yet, in 2014, we were here, marching together, representing our families and our countries. My thanks also go to Gabor Gordon for his organization of this inspiring event.

André Goodfriend with representatives of civil societies.

Photograph taken by the embassy photographer.

In September 2013, President Obama, consistent with supporting open government and transparency, launched "Stand with Civil Society," a global call to action to support, defend, and sustain civil society amid a rising tide of restrictions on its operations globally. Within Hungary, the challenges faced by civil society organizations were particularly daunting, leading the US Mission to the OSCE, on June 19, 2014, to issue a statement on "Intimidation of Civil Society and Media in Hungary". Among other programs to support civil society and democracy, in September 2014, we invited Hungarian media to discuss with representatives of a broad range of Hungarian civil society organizations, their work, the value they bring to a democratic society and the challenges they were facing.

André Goodfriend with Veronika Móra, October 9, 2014, in Budapest, at the press conference of the US embassy. Veronika Móra is the Director at the Ökotárs Foundation – the Hungarian Environmental Partnership Foundation. André Goodfriend: Currently the situation with Ökotárs has become even more of a crisis. The Hungarian government let the full Norwegian contribution disappear lest Ökotárs be given the possibility to coordinate the distribution of a fraction of the total among the civil applicants.

Photograph taken by the embassy photographer.

Following a September 24, 2014, speech by President Obama at the Clinton Global Initiative in which he said "…From Hungary to Egypt, endless regulations and overt intimidation increasingly target civil society…" the Foreign Ministry asked me to come to the Ministry and explain why the US president would say such a thing. I did, noting the raids on the offices of Hungarian civil society organizations (CSOs), as well as other actions taken against them. In October, Veronika Móra and I presented the findings of the USAID-commissioned 2013 CSO Sustainability Index which showed the deteriorating status of civil society in Hungary in terms of available funds, advocacy and legal status. Veronika Móra's organization, Ökotárs, compiled the Hungary chapter of the report. It's worth noting that while we were pointing to the decline in overall CSO sustainability from a relatively good score of 2.7 in 2005 (on a declining scale of 1 to 7) to a more marginal score of 3.2 in 2013, since that time Hungary's score has fallen even more precipitously to 4.0 in the 2021 report. (https://csosi.org/?region=EUROPE)

André Goodfriend, 2014, in front of the entrance to the former American Military Cemetery. There is no longer an American Military Cemetery in Újbuda because the United States brought back all remains of fallen Americans to America. The mural of the US flag is decaying (it has 48 stars).
From André Goodfriend's Archives.

In November 2014, as the 11th hour on the 11th day of the 11th month, marking the end of WWI (and Veterans' Day in the US) approached, I sought out the place that, for a short time, had been the final resting place for members of the American armed forces who had died during the bombing of Budapest. The bodies had long since been repatriated to the US, but the former cemetery still remained a peaceful place in which it was possible to reflect on sacrifice and the aftermath of armed conflict. I understand that, in the years since my 2014 visit, plans have been made to remove the remaining American symbols from the former cemetery and turn the venue into a park. Time moves forward. The bodies of those who perished are now elsewhere, and the ground is again a place for the living. Like so many other places I've visited, people with whom I've spoken, walls I've touched, weathered stones on which I've walked, being in a physical space creates a tangible connection that I appreciate and respect.

André Goodfriend, December 13, 2014, at the memorial "Shoes on the Bank of the Danube" by Can Togay and Gyula Pauer (2005) in downtown Budapest. *From André Goodfriend's Archives.*

Much like my reflection on the tangible connection that comes with being in a physical space, the same can be said with regard to visiting the *Shoes on the Bank of the Danube* memorial. The nature of the memorial, empty shoes, the silent aftermath of a heart-wrenching atrocity in a serenely beautiful bend of the Danube, can't help but connect the present-day visitor viscerally with the events that took place on that spot. The memorial was just a few minutes' walk from the embassy, and I visited there often—to reflect, to see the impact of the memorial on others, to try to reconcile the beauty of the location with the brutal inhumanity of the history. Each change in weather brought a different mood to the scene, and a different connection with the past. In some ways, it also touched on challenges of openness and knowing your own history. Despite knowing what we have done in the past, we cannot rule out doing it again in the future. Despite knowing what is happening in the present, we cannot be sure that we would take the action we have told ourselves rationally is morally right.

André Goodfriend with the Hungarian conductor and composer Ivan Fischer, December 27, 2014, in Budapest.

From André Goodfriend's Archives.

Ivan Fischer is inspirational in his interweaving of music, life and the world around us. We've only spoken a couple times, one time being captured here at the end of 2014; but to my mind, he exemplifies making art a part of life, using life to inspire music, and using music to inspire our lives.

André Goodfriend and George Konrad (in the middle) and András Kovács, January 1, 2015, in Budapest. András Kovács is a Hungarian sociologist whose main area of research is contemporary antisemitism and Jews in post-World War II Hungary. George (György) Konrad (1933–2019) was a Hungarian novelist and sociologist, and internationally acclaimed author. *From André Goodfriend's Archives.*

By the beginning of 2015, when this picture was taken, I'd had wonderful opportunities to talk with people throughout the range of Hungarian society, having my own preconceptions challenged and occasionally challenging those of others, while at the same time trying to integrate into conversations that had begun long before I had arrived and that were continuing long after I left. While I hadn't had a prior opportunity to speak with Konrad, I had read several of András Kovács's studies prior to my arrival in Hungary and we'd spoken on numerous occasions about the nature of Hungarian society, as well as concepts of inclusion and exclusion.

The infamous memorial of the 1944 German occupation of Hungary, which was meant to mask Hungary's participation in the Holocaust. As an artistic creation it is low-level and in poor taste. There is a counter memorial in its front, consisting of numerous mementoes gathered and exhibited. This is on Szabadság (Liberty) Square in downtown Budapest. The building in the background is the Hungarian National Bank. Further to the left, unseen, is the US embassy.

André Goodfriend took this picture in 2015.

The memorial to the victims of the 1944 German occupation of Hungary was just a few steps away from the embassy, and I couldn't help but walk past it nearly every day. In some ways it and the outcry it stirred up were symbolic of the challenges Hungary faced in reconciling with its own history and defining itself as a nation. It also encapsulates many of the elements of the discussion on open government and transparency. From the stealthy manner in which the plan for the memorial was announced to the selection of its design, to the promises made and broken for consultation, to its unceremonious unveiling in the dead of night, the memorial promoted a message that divided more than united Hungarian society around its interpretation of history and its definition of the nation that was victimized during WWII. In an embassy statement issued on April 22, 2014, shortly after the memorial was unveiled, we highlighted the importance of engagement, open dialogue and transparency saying, "Constructive engagement between a government and its citizens is a hallmark of good democratic governance, and we were encouraged by promises of dialogue. Following the government's election victory, genuine dialogue would demonstrate the government's commitment to discussing openly and transparently important issues even with those who may at times disagree with the government position."

Istvan Hargittai, PhD, DSc, is a physical chemist and Professor Emeritus (active) at the Budapest University of Technology and Economics. He is a member of the Hungarian Academy of Sciences and the Academia Europaea (London) and foreign member of the Norwegian Academy of Science and Letters. He is Dr.h.c. of Moscow State University, the University of North Carolina, and the Russian Academy of Sciences. He is the Founding Editor-in-Chief of *Structural Chemistry*, a Springer Nature international research journal in its 34th year of publication. He has authored and edited numerous books about structural chemistry, the history of science, the nature of scientific discovery, memorials of scientists, conversations with famous scientists, and other topics. His books have appeared in English, Hungarian, Russian, German, Swedish, Italian, Japanese, Chinese, and in the Farsi language.

M. André Goodfriend retired from the U.S. Department of State in 2022 as a member of the Senior Foreign Service with the rank of Minister Counselor after a career lasting over three decades. Serving as Director of the State Department's Office of eDiplomacy, Mr. Goodfriend coordinated preparation of the State Department's Open Government Plan and worked to facilitate the conduct of diplomacy with technologies, promoting knowledge sharing and transparency. In Budapest, Hungary, in the absence of an ambassador, he served as Chargé d'Affaires a.i., engaging in an open conversation on approaches to implementing shared values. As Consul General in Damascus during the years prior to the closure of the U.S. embassy, Mr. Goodfriend utilized increased public engagement and collaborative effort to safeguard the welfare of the U.S. citizen community in an increasingly hostile environment. Other overseas assignments have included Israel, India, Russia, and the UK. Born in California and raised in Arizona, Mr. Goodfriend has studied Hungarian, Hebrew, French, Russian, Greek (classical and modern), Spanish, Hindi, Arabic, and Yiddish.

Also by Istvan Hargittai

I. Hargittai, B. Hargittai, *Brilliance in Exile: Diaspora of Hungarian Scientists from John von Neumann to Katalin Karikó* (Central European University Press 2023)

B. Hargittai, I. Hargittai, *Quotable John von Neumann: Thoughts of a Great Scientist* (Neumann Society 2023)

I. Hargittai, M. Hargittai, *Science in London: A Guide to Memorials* (Springer Nature 2021)

I. Hargittai, *Mosaic of a Scientific Life* (Springer Nature, 2020)

I. Hargittai, M. Hargittai, *Moscow Scientific: Memorials of a Research Empire* (World Scientific, 2019)

B. Hargittai, ed., *Culture and Art of Scientific Discoveries: A Selection of István Hargittai's Writings* (Springer Nature, 2019)

I. Hargittai, M. Hargittai, *New York Scientific: A Culture of Inquiry, Knowledge, and Learning* (Oxford University Press, 2017)

B. Hargittai, I. Hargittai, *Wisdom of the Martians of Science: In Their Own Words with Commentaries* (World Scientific, 2016)

I. Hargittai, M. Hargittai, *Budapest Scientific: A Guidebook* (Oxford University Press, 2015)

B. Hargittai, M. Hargittai, I. Hargittai, *Great Minds: Reflections of 111 Top Scientists* (Oxford University Press, 2014)

I. Hargittai, *Buried Glory: Portraits of Soviet Scientists* (Oxford University Press, 2013)

I. Hargittai, *Drive and Curiosity: What Fuels the Passion for Science* (Prometheus, 2011)

I. Hargittai, *Judging Edward Teller: A Closer Look at One of the Most Influential Scientists of the Twentieth Century* (Prometheus, 2010)

I. Hargittai, M. Hargittai, *Symmetry through the Eyes of a Chemist* (3rd Edition, Springer, 2009, 2010)

M. Hargittai, I. Hargittai, *Visual Symmetry* (World Scientific, 2009)

I. Hargittai, *The DNA Doctor: Candid Conversations with James D. Watson* (World Scientific, 2007)

I. Hargittai, *The Martians of Science: Five Physicists Who Changed the Twentieth Century* (Oxford University Press, 2006, 2008)

I. Hargittai, *The Tragedy of Edward Teller* (Hungarian Academy of Sciences, 2005)

I. Hargittai, *Our Lives: Encounters of a Scientist* (Akadémiai Kiadó, 2004)

I. Hargittai, *The Road to Stockholm: Nobel Prizes, Science, and Scientists* (Oxford University Press, 2002, 2003)

B. Hargittai, I. Hargittai, M. Hargittai, *Candid Science I–VI: Conversations with Famous Scientists* (Imperial College Press, 2000–2006)

I. Hargittai, M. Hargittai, *In Our Own Image: Personal Symmetry in Discovery* (Kluwer/Plenum, 2000; Springer, 2012)

I. Hargittai, M. Hargittai, *Symmetry: A Unifying Concept* (Shelter, 1994; Random House, 1996)

Index of Names

Ingram Content Group UK Ltd.
Milton Keynes UK
UKHW021306180723
425352UK00035B/445